100 THINGS
CAVALIERS FANS
SHOULD KNOW & DO
BEFORE THEY DIE

100 THINGS CAVALIERS FANS SHOULD KNOW & DO BEFORE THEY DIE

Bob Finnan

TRIUMPH
BOOKS

This book is available in quantity at special discounts for your group or organization. For further information, contact:

Triumph Books LLC
814 North Franklin Street
Chicago, IL 60610
(312) 337-0747
www.triumphbooks.com

Printed in the United States of America

ISBN: 978-1-62937-190-0
Design by Patricia Frey
Editorial production by Alex Lubertozzi
Photos courtesy of AP Images

To my loving wife Susan and my four children,
Alyson, Lyndsey, Jill, and Tom

Contents

Foreword

In today's world, the Cavaliers are all about LeBron James. The entire team revolves around the three-time NBA champion and four-time Most Valuable Player. However, there has been an interesting cast of characters through the years who wore the Wine & Gold. In this book, *100 Things Cavaliers Fans Should Know and Do Before They Die*, author Bob Finnan chronicles the team from its inception to present day. He takes you on a journey of many of the good times and bad.

It started when Nick Mileti founded the team in 1970 and the original Cavs played at Cleveland Arena. I joined the team the following year as the No. 1 pick in the 1971 NBA Draft. I've spent what seems like my entire adult life with the franchise. I played nine seasons in Cleveland, including the Miracle of Richfield season of 1975–1976. That will always be a special time in my heart.

Finnan chronicles numerous stories from that era, from adding Hall of Fame center Nate Thurmond to the disappointment that came from Jim Chones' foot injury. Playing for Hall of Fame coach Bill Fitch wasn't always easy, but I'll never forget it.

I never wanted to leave Cleveland, but I was picked by the Dallas Mavericks in the expansion draft on May 28, 1980. I played only eight games with the Mavericks before being sold to the Washington Bullets on November 6, 1980. Even though I was able to return to the Washington, D.C., area where I grew up, that didn't last long, either. My time with the Bullets was over after 39 games. My career ended after the 1980–1981 season.

With the exception of a few years away from the team, I've been a part of the Cavs ever since. Even after I retired and worked in the packing business in Indianapolis, I still called Cleveland my home.

My broadcast partner, Fred McLeod, labeled me "Mr. Cavalier" when we were paired together in the Fox Sports Ohio television booth in 2007. It has stuck. I take being Mr. Cavalier very seriously. To represent the franchise in an unofficial way, it's a big responsibility. I take it seriously. I don't shrug it off. It's amazing how it has stuck with me. It doesn't matter if I'm in Cleveland or out of town, I proudly carry that moniker with me.

I love being a television analyst. It keeps me involved with something I love. I can express myself and show my passion for the game. Of course, getting to watch LeBron, Kyrie Irving, and Kevin Love on a nightly basis isn't too bad, either. This is something I enjoy. I want to do it as long as I can. In this profession, you continue to learn things. You have to stay open to constructive criticism. It's a learning process.

I'm so thankful the Cavs will finally get to raise a championship banner in Quicken Loans Arena. That's icing on the cake. We all deserve at least one.

—Austin Carr

1 Cavs Win 2016 NBA Championship

Grown men broke down and cried.

Finally, before many of them died, they got to experience another sports championship in Cleveland. The Cavaliers topped the Golden State Warriors 93–89 in Game 7 of the NBA Finals on June 19, 2016, to capture their first NBA title and end the city of Cleveland's 52-year championship drought.

The curse is over.

Cleveland will no longer be the butt of national jokes about its sports futility. It hadn't experienced a championship since 1964 when the Browns blanked the Baltimore Colts 27–0 for the NFL crown. Before that, the 1948 Indians won the World Series four games to two over the Boston Braves.

That left a lot of barren years in between.

Cavs forward LeBron James promised that he'd bring a championship to Cleveland when he returned in the summer of 2014. When it finally happened—giving many in northeast Ohio the best Father's Day gift ever—the 31-year-old James fell to the Oracle Arena floor and cried.

In postgame interviews that were aired over Oracle's public-address system, James said, "This is for you, Cleveland."

It touched off a week-long celebration in Cleveland and the state of Ohio. An estimated 1.3 million people attended the championship parade and rally June 22 in downtown Cleveland.

Facing a 3–1 deficit in the NBA Finals, the Cavs roared back to win the last three games, including two at Oracle, to win the coveted crown. The Cavs are the only team in NBA history to come back from a 3–1 deficit in the Finals. Thirty-two other teams had tried and failed to storm back from that deep hole.

The turning point in the series might have been with two minutes, 48 seconds left in Game 4. The Warriors were on their way to a 108–97 victory at Quicken Loans Arena when Golden State forward Draymond Green got tangled up with James and hit the floor. James stepped over Green, which seemed to provoke the Warriors' rising star. Green reached up and hit James in the groin. They were given a double technical, but the NBA's Kiki Vandeweghe reviewed the play. His hit to James' groin was upgraded to a flagrant foul, putting him over the limit of four for flagrant foul points in the postseason, meaning an automatic suspension for the following game.

"The cumulative points system is designed to deter flagrant fouls in our game," Vandeweghe said. "While Draymond Green's actions in Game 4 do not merit a suspension as a stand-alone act, the number of flagrant points he has earned triggers a suspension in Game 5."

Green had angered the Oklahoma City Thunder in the Western Conference finals with a kick to center Steven Adams' groin. Somehow, that didn't necessitate a suspension.

The play that some called dirty also seemed to light a fire under James, something even the cocky Warriors didn't want to do. In the last three games of the series, James averaged 36.3 points, including back-to-back 41-point games.

For the series, the MVP averaged 29.7 points, 11.3 rebounds, and 8.9 assists. He finished off Golden State in Game 7 with a triple-double: 27 points, 11 rebounds, and 11 assists, to go with three blocks and two steals.

In Game 5, Warriors center Andrew Bogut suffered a knee injury in the third quarter of the Warriors' 112–97 loss at Oracle Arena. He landed awkwardly on his left leg trying to block a shot by Cavs guard J.R. Smith. The 7′ Bogut had made a huge impact in Game 2 with five blocked shots. He missed the final two games of the series.

2016 NBA Finals

Game 1 — June 2 (at Golden State): Warriors 104, Cavs 89
Game 2 — June 5 (at Golden State): Warriors 110, Cavs 77
Game 3 — June 8 (at Cleveland): Cavs 120, Warriors 90
Game 4 — June 10 (at Cleveland): Warriors 108, Cavs 97
Game 5 — June 13 (at Golden State): Cavs 112, Warriors 97
Game 6 — June 16 (at Cleveland): Cavs 115, Warriors 101
Game 7 — June 19 (at Golden State): Cavs 93, Warriors 89
(Cavs win series 4–3)

That wasn't the only major injury in the NBA Finals. Cavs power forward Kevin Love suffered a concussion in Game 2, which forced him to miss the following game while going through the league's concussion protocol. Love was elbowed in the back of the head by Warriors forward Harrison Barnes while going for a rebound with five minutes remaining in the second quarter of Game 2. No foul was called on the play, which left Love lying on the floor, holding his head. He later came back in the game and hit a three-pointer. The Cavs' medical staff didn't detect any concussion symptoms, but Love later became disoriented and was taken to the locker room.

"When we came back out in the third quarter, I could see in a timeout he looked kind of woozy," Cavs coach Tyronn Lue told ESPN. "He went back on the floor for a second, and then we had to get him off the floor."

Love wasn't much of a factor in the series until Game 7 when he finished with nine points and a team-high 14 rebounds.

The Cavs grabbed the momentum of the series in Game 5, as James and guard Kyrie Irving became the first teammates in NBA history to score 41 or more points in the same game in the NBA Finals.

"Our coaching staff gave us a great game plan and, as one of the leaders of the team, we just went out and executed," James said. "You've got a guy like this [Irving], who is very special. It's probably one of the greatest performances I've ever seen live. To put on the show that he did, you just go out and follow the keys and play winning basketball, and we did that tonight."

Unfortunately for the Warriors, they couldn't stop the Cavs' onslaught.

The Cavs' rallying cry was to stretch the series to Game 7, at which point anything could happen. With a player like James on the roster, that can help nullify home-court advantage.

Game 7 was a classic. The Cavs' defense in the game—and the series, really—was outstanding. They held the Warriors scoreless in the last 4:39 of the game. Warriors guard Klay Thompson's layup knotted the score at 89. The two teams were tied at 89 for what seemed like an eternity.

Two plays followed in the last two minutes that became instant classics and helped define the Cavs' moxie. Warriors swingman Andre Iguodala attacked the basket with 1:50 to play on a Golden State fast break. James' chase-down blocks have become legendary in Cleveland through the years, but none were on such a big stage and in such a key juncture in the biggest game in franchise history. He came out of nowhere to block Iguodala's layup. At first glance, it seemed like he pinned it to the backboard, which would have been goaltending. But he blocked it an instant before hitting the glass to thwart a potential go-ahead basket. Further scrutiny of the play showed that guard J.R. Smith forced Iguodala to alter his shot. That allowed James to catch up to the play and make the biggest defensive play in the series.

Cavs coach Tyronn Lue got on his team at halftime of Game 7, as they trailed by seven points. "He told us, 'We've got 24 minutes,'" James told *USA Today.* "'We've got to play as hard as we've ever played in the next 24 minutes.'"

James said Lue singled him out in the locker room. "'It starts with you,'" Lue told James. "He got on me a little bit. [He] told me to pick up everything I've been doing and give even more effort. We all responded."

LeBron James makes "The Block"—rejecting Warriors swingman Andre Iguodala's layup attempt with the score tied 89–89 and under two minutes to go in Game 7 of the 2016 NBA Finals.

Getting Under the MVP's Skin

The Cavs made a concentrated effort to put the defensive clamps on Warriors guard Stephen Curry in the 2016 NBA Finals. They grabbed him. They bumped him. They banged him around. They were overly aggressive with the two-time Most Valuable Player.

It all caught up with the 6'3", 190-pounder in Game 6 at Quicken Loans Arena. Curry fouled out with 4:22 left in the game. His frustrations boiled over and he threw his mouthpiece into the crowd. He was immediately ejected for the first time in his NBA career.

According to multiple reports, the mouthpiece hit Andrew Forbes, the son of minority Cavs owner Nate Forbes. Curry apologized to Forbes, and the two shook hands. "It's all good," Forbes told ESPN's Tom Haberstroh. "It just hit me, and I was like, 'Who? What?' I was just cheering, being a fan. I don't even know where he was throwing it....He was good about it."

Warriors coach Steve Kerr and Curry were both fined $25,000 by the NBA after the 115–101 loss. "I'm happy he threw his mouthpiece," Kerr said in his postgame comments. "He should be upset. Look, it's the Finals and everybody's competing out there. There are fouls on every play. It's a physical game....If they're going to let Cleveland grab and hold these guys constantly on their cuts, and then you're going to call these ticky-tack fouls on the MVP of the league to foul him out, I don't agree with that."

They were upset with many of Curry's six fouls. Kerr, the league's Coach of the Year, took issue with three of them, calling them "absolutely ridiculous.""Let me be clear: we did not lose because of the officiating," Kerr said. "They totally out-played us, and Cleveland deserved to win. But those three of the six fouls were incredibly inappropriate calls for anybody, much less the MVP of the league."

Kerr even called out official Jason Philips by name on the sixth foul on Curry. That caused Curry to throw his mouthpiece. "I've thrown my mouthpiece before," he said. "I usually aim at the scorer's table. I was off aim. [I] definitely didn't mean to throw it at a fan. That was definitely not where I wanted to take out my frustration."

Curry hadn't fouled out of a game since December 13, 2013.

"It got the best of me," he said.

Even Curry's wife, Ayesha, barged her way into the news. She became an Internet sensation after she commented on Twitter: "I've lost all respect sorry this is absolutely rigged for money...or ratings [I'm] not sure which. I won't be silent. Just saw it live. (Sorry)." She later deleted the tweet and apologized.

Things got even worse for Ayesha. Her father almost got arrested at The Q that night when he was mistaken for another man by NBA security. Security was heightened and on the lookout for a man who didn't have proper credentials and had been sneaking into sporting events.

Ayesha said her father was racially profiled in a story filed by Marc J. Spears of The Undefeated. Apparently, her father had a resemblance to the man.

"It's been a long night for me," she tweeted.

Curry was briefed by an NBA official about the situation with his father-in-law.

"I was just kind of debriefed on what the security thought happened with some guy that poses with fake credentials and gets backstage at a lot of events, the NBA Finals and all that stuff," Curry told The Undefeated. "They kind of profiled my father-in-law and thought he was him. They threatened to arrest him before they checked out his credentials. It's kind of been an emotional and tough night all the way around. That was kind of a traumatic situation where [Ayesha's] dad almost got arrested. So it was kind of a tough situation to deal with in a hostile environment. All in all, it's just a game. I hope that everybody is all right."

Ayesha Curry also took to social media to complain that a bus carrying the Warriors' friends and family was delayed before Game 6. She implied it was a tactic being used by the Cavs, which a team source denied. She said she arrived to The Q at the start of the game.

Beyonce and Jay Z, two of the many celebrities in attendance, were also caught in traffic congestion before the game.

Speaking of mouthpieces, ESPN's Darren Rovell said a game-used Curry mouthpiece—not the one he tossed in Game 6—will be auctioned off by a California-based company, SPC Auctions, in August 2016. It's expected to sell for around $5,000.

"Steph Curry has given more life to mouthguards than any player in history," vice president of SPC auctions Dan Imler told ESPN. "The way he flips it in and out of his mouth has become part of watching him during a game."

Irving put the exclamation point on the series with a clutch three-pointer with 53 seconds remaining. His 25-foot, pull-up jumper over Stephen Curry proved to be the dagger in Game 7. Irving outplayed the league's two-time MVP in the NBA Finals. He averaged 27.1 points, 3.9 rebounds, and 3.9 assists in the series. Curry averaged 22.6 points, 4.9 rebounds and 3.7 assists.

The Cavs held potent Golden State to an average of 99.86 points in the NBA Finals, which was significant. The Warriors were first

Most-Watched, Tweeted Finals

The 2016 NBA Finals was an epic seven-game series that left fans glued to their seats. The NBA announced it also set records in television viewership, along with social, digital, and retail platforms.

The seven-game series was the most-watched NBA Finals in ABC history and most-watched overall since 1998. It averaged 20.22 million viewers per game. Game 7 averaged 31.02 million viewers—peaking with 44.81 million viewers—the third-most-watched NBA game ever.

A record 5.2 billion impressions and 800 million video views were generated during the Finals across social platforms. The end of Game 7 amassed 337,000 tweets per minute, the top-tweeted moment in Finals history and most-tweeted U.S. sports moment in 2016.

The Cavaliers-Warriors matchup was the most-talked about NBA Finals ever on Facebook, with a record 43 million people posting, liking, sharing, and commenting more than 269 million times.

NBA.com and the NBA app tallied a record 1.9 billion page views and 1.4 billion video views, eclipsing the previous records of 1.1 billion and 400 million, respectively, set during the 2015 Finals.

The day after Game 7, NBAStore.com had its highest sales day in store history, breaking the previous record set last season.

in the NBA during the regular season with 114.9 points per game, 48.7 percent shooting from the field, and 41.6 percent from the three-point line. The Warriors' 73 wins during the regular season were the most ever, as were their 88 wins combined in the regular and postseason. Golden State started the season 24–0.

When the Warriors took a 3–1 lead in the Finals, not many people gave the Cavs much of a chance. "We just accomplished something that no team has ever done," James said. "That's all the credit to my teammates and the coaching staff. They were unbelievable. Just knowing what our city has been through, northeast Ohio has been through, as far as our sports and everything for the last 50-plus years. You could look back to the Earnest Byner fumble, [John] Elway going 99 yards, to Jose Mesa not being able to close out in the bottom of the ninth, to the Cavs [going] to the Finals—I was on

Surrounded by his teammates, LeBron James breaks down holding on to the 2016 NBA Championship Trophy after the Cavs beat the Golden State Warriors 93–89 in Game 7 to win Cleveland's first NBA title and the city's first championship of any kind since 1964. James was also named the Finals MVP.

that team—in 2007, us getting swept, and then last year, us losing 4–2. And so many more stories."

James said the Cavs won the title for their fans.

"Our fans, they ride or die, no matter what's been going on, no matter the Browns, the Indians, the Cavs, and all other sports teams, they continue to support us," James said. "And for us to be able to end this, end this drought, our fans deserve it. They deserve it. And it was for them."

Cavs general manager David Griffin said three plays will live in Cleveland folklore forever: James' block, Irving's three-pointer, and Love's defense on Curry in the closing seconds.

Irving modestly credited James with making his moment possible. "There is no shot without the block," he said.

2 2003 NBA Draft Lottery

The buildup for the 2003 NBA Draft lottery was in the works for more than a year. The Cavs went out of their way to tank the 2002–2003 season to make sure they got a shot at LeBron James, a once-in-a-generation type of player.

The Akron St. Vincent–St. Mary High School star was probably better than half the players in the NBA by the time he reached his senior year in high school. The Cavs felt it was imperative they gave themselves the best opportunity for the No. 1 pick. In actuality, they couldn't have gone wrong if they had any of the top five selections—unless they were the Detroit Pistons. They had the No. 2 pick and wasted it on European big man Darko Milicic.

The Cavs finished with a 17–65 record during the 2002–2003 season, tied with the Denver Nuggets for the worst record in the league. Both teams had a 22.5 percent chance at the top pick in the draft lottery on May 22, 2003, in Secaucus, New Jersey. The top of the draft was littered with Hall of Fame talent that included James, Syracuse forward Carmelo Anthony (third to Denver), Georgia Tech forward/center Chris Bosh (fourth to Toronto), and Marquette guard Dwyane Wade (fifth to Miami).

But make no bones about it, the teams at the top of the draft all wanted to get their hands on James. That included Memphis Grizzlies president Jerry West. The Grizzlies ended up with the No. 2 pick in the lottery, but were forced to forfeit the selection to the Pistons for a previous trade for Otis Thorpe.

"When you get down to these situations with a player of the magnitude at one or two in the draft, it would have been an enormous addition to our team—enormous," West told *Sports Illustrated.* "I think there are three or four kids in this draft that are going to be tremendous NBA players, and more importantly for the city of Memphis and the Grizzlies coaching staff, if we'd have gotten the No. 1 pick we would have gotten a real special player."

The Cavs had been able to watch James' development as the most complete high school player in the nation. St. Vincent–St. Mary High is only about 30 miles south of Cleveland. James also came to Gund Arena and worked out against the Cavs and other professional players, which might have cemented the Cavs' devotion to him.

Nerves were frayed on the night of the lottery. Cavs owner Gordon Gund came out and ate with the media a few hours before the prime-time event. That had never happened before. James had rented a hotel suite at the Radisson Hotel in downtown Akron. Friends, family, and his management team were on hand. He had to be feeling pretty good that day, since he signed a $90 million contract with Nike—the most lucrative shoe deal in history—the night before. "LeBron and everyone were nervous," James' agent, Aaron Goodwin, told ESPN. "There were a lot of people there, but you could tell they were enjoying it."

Once the lottery started to unfold, it came down to the last three teams. The Cavs were still in the running. "When it went to commercial and we knew the top three were Denver, Memphis, and Cleveland, I just had a feeling that I'm going to stay home," James told ESPN. "I could hear the chatter starting in the room. They were getting excited."

Goodwin, James' agent from 2003 to 2005, could feel that excitement. "By then, we all wanted Cleveland," he said. "It was going to be a fairy tale."

Finally, the NBA's deputy commissioner, Russ Granik, opened the last envelope and held up a Cavs logo. It touched off a wild celebration in New Jersey and Ohio. James said he was going to light up Cleveland like Las Vegas.

The Cavs were hosting a lottery party at Champp's in suburban Valley View. The emotions of the night were too much for Cavs announcer Austin Carr. "One of my only and biggest regrets about being in New Jersey at the actual lottery," Cavs senior vice president of communications Tad Carper told the *Cleveland Plain Dealer*, "was seeing a video of the reaction at the lottery party event here with AC leaning over and crying on Mike Snyder's shoulder. It almost made me cry myself when I saw it."

The Cavs were floundering at the time. Carr knew what getting a player of James' magnitude would mean to the team. "It was a very emotional night," Carr said, "and it got to me."

3 The Decision

The Cavs lost in the 2007 and 2015 NBA Finals. Neither was as devastating as LeBron James' announcement that he was "taking his talents to South Beach." James earned two NBA championship rings in his four years with the Miami Heat. However, in the process, his name turned to mud in Northeast Ohio.

James made the announcement on *The Decision*, which aired on ESPN, that he was leaving the Cavs on July 8, 2010, to sign with the Heat as a free agent. "I'm going to take my talents to South Beach and join the Miami Heat," he said on national TV. "I feel like it's going to give me the best opportunity to win and to win for multiple years, and not only just to win in the regular season or just to win five games in a row or three games in a row. I want to be able to win championships. And I feel like I can compete down there."

He joined forces with Dwyane Wade and Chris Bosh and earned NBA titles in 2012 and 2013. Leading up to the decision, James took the basketball world through the dog-and-pony show of meeting with six teams at the IMG building on East Ninth Street in Downtown Cleveland. Miami, the New Jersey Nets, New York Knicks, the Los Angeles Clippers, Chicago Bulls, and hometown Cavs made presentations to James. Those were the teams that had the salary cap space to sign James to a maximum contract.

The Cavs felt good about their chances of retaining James. Not only could they offer him $30 million more than any other team over the length of a max contract, they could also offer an additional year (six years compared to five). Besides the dollars and cents, they felt they had the necessary pieces around him to challenge for an NBA title.

Cavs owner Dan Gilbert, coach Byron Scott, general manager Chris Grant, and assistant GM Lance Blanks made the pitch to James. They showed him an animated video in the style of *Family Guy*—one of James' favorite TV shows.

Perhaps they should have taken more of a serious approach.

James was joined in the meetings by business manager Maverick Carter, close friend Randy Mims, and agent Leon Rose. He shocked the world when he shunned the Cavs and decided to join the Heat. He had discussed this "collaboration" with Wade and Bosh for weeks, sources said. "I didn't want to make an emotional decision," James said on ESPN. "I wanted to do what was best for LeBron James and what would make him happy. This is a business, and I had seven great years in Cleveland. I hope the fans understand; maybe they won't."

They didn't. Fans burned No. 23 Cavs jerseys in the streets after *The Decision.*

Minutes before James' announcement, his close friend, Rich Paul, called Grant to inform him of the crushing decision. Paul, a Cleveland native, later became James' agent. The Cavs had remained confident James would return home up until the last few hours. Gilbert wasn't even in town. He was reportedly attending a millionaires' retreat in Idaho. That didn't prevent him from springing into action after James' decision with "The Letter," which was emailed out later that night.

Gilbert admitted later it was actually the second take on the letter. The first draft was toned down a few decibels. He was fined $100,000 by NBA commissioner David Stern for the letter's contents. Stern also criticized the way James handled free agency.

James' first trip back to Cleveland on December 2, 2010, was a sight to see. Cavs fans were out for vengeance…and a pound of flesh. James just shudders to think about that game.

After rejoining the Cavs for the 2014–2015 season, he made his first return trip to Miami on December 25, 2014. "I don't get involved," he said. "My job is to go down there and live in the moment."

ESPN analyst Hubie Brown said because James took the Heat to four consecutive NBA Finals appearances, including two championships, the fans should honor him. "The only reason he was booed in Cleveland is because they wanted him to stay there," Brown said.

The Heat honored James with a video tribute. "I would be stunned if [James] did not get a standing ovation, and also that it stayed a standing ovation for a while, mainly because of what he accomplished while he was there and how far he took that situation," Brown said. "Not only the rings, but also the sellout crowds on a nightly basis, the total excitement of the four seasons."

Brown said James evolved into the best player in the NBA when he went to Miami. "He grew," Brown said. "His game grew. The championships were there. The Finals were there. The Olympic golds were there. So I just can't believe [he'd be booed]. I would hate to see it because I cherish the memories of what he did as an athlete, his contribution, reaching his maximum potential, and then also creating chemistry offensively and defensively for that team down there. That to me is what professional basketball and a player of his caliber is expected to do, and he did it."

The Letter

The following was released by Cavs owner Dan Gilbert on July 8, 2010, after LeBron James decided to play for Miami:

Dear Cleveland, All of Northeast Ohio, and Cleveland Cavaliers Supporters Wherever You May Be Tonight;

As you now know, our former hero, who grew up in the very region that he deserted this evening, is no longer a Cleveland Cavalier.

This was announced with a several-day, narcissistic, self-promotional build-up culminating with a national TV special of his "decision" unlike anything ever "witnessed" in the history of sports and probably the history of entertainment.

Clearly, this is bitterly disappointing to all of us.

The good news is that the ownership team and the rest of the hard-working, loyal, and driven staff over here at your hometown Cavaliers have not betrayed you nor NEVER will betray you.

There is so much more to tell you about the events of the recent past and our more than exciting future. Over the next several days and weeks, we will be communicating much of that to you.

You simply don't deserve this kind of cowardly betrayal.

You have given so much and deserve so much more.

In the meantime, I want to make one statement to you tonight:

"I PERSONALLY GUARANTEE THAT THE CLEVELAND CAVALIERS WILL WIN AN NBA CHAMPIONSHIP BEFORE THE SELF-TITLED FORMER 'KING' WINS ONE."

You can take it to the bank.

If you thought we were motivated before tonight to bring the hardware to Cleveland, I can tell you that this shameful display of selfishness and betrayal by one of our very own has shifted our "motivation" to previously unknown and previously never experienced levels.

Some people think they should go to heaven but NOT have to die to get there.

Sorry, but that's simply not how it works.

This shocking act of disloyalty from our homegrown "chosen one" sends the exact opposite lesson of what we would want our children to learn. And "who" we would want them to grow up to become.

But the good news is that this heartless and callous action can only serve as the antidote to the so-called "curse" on Cleveland, Ohio.

The self-declared former "King" will be taking the "curse" with him down south. And until he does "right" by Cleveland and Ohio, James (and the town where he plays) will unfortunately own this dreaded spell and bad karma.

Just watch.

Sleep well, Cleveland.

Tomorrow is a new and much brighter day...

I PROMISE you that our energy, focus, capital, knowledge, and experience will be directed at one thing and one thing only:

DELIVERING YOU the championship you have long deserved and is long overdue...

Dan Gilbert
Majority Owner
Cleveland Cavaliers

4 First Trip to the NBA Finals

In 2007 the Cavs interrupted the Detroit Pistons' stranglehold on the Eastern Conference. The Pistons had advanced to the Eastern finals six consecutive years from 2003 to 2008. That included 2007, when they faced off with the Cavs.

Unlike previous years, however, the Cavs proved to be the better team, despite losing the first two games of the series. The Cavs stormed back and won the last four games of the series to advance to the NBA Finals for the first time in franchise history.

Once they arrived in the Finals opposite Western Conference champion San Antonio, the underdog Cavs made a stark realization. They just weren't ready for the bright lights and the glare. There was one other problem—and a big one at that—the Spurs were far superior to the Cavs in almost every category. They had more talent, more experience, better depth, were better coached, and had home-court advantage. It resulted in one of the most lopsided NBA Finals in history.

San Antonio swept the Cavs, four games to none, to win the 2007 NBA championship. There have been only six sweeps in the last 45 years of the NBA, dating back to the Milwaukee Bucks' four-game demolition of the Baltimore Bullets in 1971. Golden State also swept Washington in 1975, Philadelphia ran the table on the Los Angeles Lakers in 1983, Houston won four straight games over Orlando in 1995, and the Lakers dominated New Jersey in 2002.

The Cavs were just happy to be there. Some thought their triumph in the Eastern finals was an upset in itself. But that's where the excitement stopped. They weren't equipped to compete against the heavily favored Spurs once they got to the promised land.

Spurs coach Gregg Popovich centered all his defensive efforts on stopping LeBron James. He knew no one else on the Cavs roster could beat him. The Spurs had too much firepower, led by forward/center Tim Duncan, swingman Manu Ginobili, and point guard Tony Parker, the Finals' MVP. All three could be Hall of Famers when their careers are over.

The Cavs countered with a banged-up Larry Hughes, struggling center Zydrunas Ilgauskas, and power forward Drew Gooden. Hughes, signed to a monstrous free-agent deal in the summer of 2006, managed just one field goal in the series. He started the first

LeBron James tries to score between the Spurs' Tim Duncan (21) and Bruce Bowen during the Cavs' loss in the decisive Game 4 of the 2007 NBA Finals.

two games at point guard, and rookie Daniel "Boobie" Gibson replaced him in the final two. Gibson shot 1-of-10 from the field in Game 3. Hughes had a torn plantar fascia in his left foot, which

2007 NBA Finals
Game 1 — June 7 (at San Antonio): Spurs 85, Cavs 76
Game 2 — June 10 (at San Antonio): Spurs 103, Cavs 92
Game 3 — June 12 (at Cleveland): Spurs 75, Cavs 72
Game 4 — June 14 (at Cleveland): Spurs 83, Cavs 82
(Spurs win series 4–0)

severely limited his effectiveness. He had to get cortisone shots just to get on the court. "It was pretty much a dead foot," he recalled.

Both Hughes and Gibson got shredded by Parker, who slashed his way to the basket at ease. He won MVP honors after leading all scorers in the Finals with a sparkling 24.5-point average. He was practically unstoppable.

The Spurs sagged on James and dared him to shoot from the perimeter. He shot 35.6 percent from the floor and 20 percent from the three-point line in the series. ABC television executives were probably already disappointed when two small markets like San Antonio and Cleveland made it to the Finals. Combined with the Cavs' poor showing in the series, the Finals produced very low TV ratings nationally.

5 Miracle of Richfield

The Cavs were primed to win a championship. After all those years of losing teams—some downright pitiful—the Cavs were ready to make that next step. Coach Bill Fitch assembled a championship roster that was 10 deep with legitimate talent. They made the playoffs for the first time after winning the Central Division title, and the Richfield Coliseum was electric.

Perhaps the most exciting aspect of the 1975–1976 season was the fans. They came in droves, they were loyal, and they were loud. They set an NBA playoff record with 21,564 at the Coliseum for Game 7 against the Washington Bullets. The Eastern Conference semifinal series went right down to the wire. The Cavs slipped past the Bullets by the slimmest of margins. Guard Dick Snyder's shot went high off the glass and through the hoop at the buzzer to win Game 7. Fans at the Coliseum tore the basket down.

The season before, they missed the playoffs by one game—one last-second shot, Cavs guard Austin Carr said. They were beaten by the Kansas City Kings on April 6, 1975, 95–94, which knocked them out of the playoff race.

They weren't going to be denied in the 1975–1976 season, forever after known as the Miracle of Richfield. After a slow start, Fitch made perhaps the most important move of the season. He traded for aging center Nate Thurmond. "We had a good mix of personalities and talent," Carr said. "Nate Thurmond was our anchor."

Carr was no longer the same player he once was when he came into the league. The injuries had taken their toll on the pure scorer. "I found a niche," he said. "We all developed a niche for ourselves. We had a good mixture coming off the bench. [Celtics coach] Tommy Heinsohn coined us 'instant offense.'"

Carr and forward Campy Russell provided the firepower off the bench. Bobby "Bingo" Smith, Jimmy Cleamons, and Jim Chones took care of the rest. "When we got Nate, we never looked back," Carr said. "We needed someone to show us how good we were. He woke us up. He made us realize we had the talent and to go out and believe in ourselves."

Carr said they were confident the Cavs could win a championship. All they had to do was get past the Boston Celtics in the Eastern Conference Finals. They figured the Phoenix Suns would be waiting for them in the NBA Finals, and they had handled them twice that year. "We were looking forward to the battle with Boston," he said. "Boston was the kingpin in the league with JoJo White and Dave Cowens. They were the darlings of the league."

That euphoric feeling ended when Chones broke a bone in his right foot two days before the start of the Eastern Finals. Instead of storming to the NBA Finals for the first time in franchise history, they were defeated by the Celtics, four games to two. Officially, the Celtics get credit for stopping the Cavs' magical postseason run. But fans in Cleveland know the real reason: Chones' unfortunate injury. When it was announced, it was a deflating feeling. "The only time I felt like that was when JFK got shot," Carr said. "It was a terrible feeling in the pit of my stomach."

Chones, a former standout at Marquette, played his first two seasons in the ABA, with the New York Nets and Carolina Cougars, respectively. The Los Angeles Lakers traded his NBA rights to the Cavs on May 17, 1974, for a 1975 first-round pick. The 6'11", 220-pound forward/center quickly became one of the Cavs' best players. During the 1975–1976 season, he averaged a career-high 15.8 points and 9.0 rebounds.

The fans started thinking about an NBA championship after the Cavs eliminated the Washington Bullets in the Eastern Conference semifinals, four games to three. However, Chones landed on a team-mate's foot in the final practice before the Celtics series. Chones told the *Cleveland Plain Dealer* the Cavs were more confident about beating Boston than they were getting past the Bullets—at least before his injury.

Chones' broken foot forced the Cavs to start aging Nate Thurmond at center and use Jim Brewer as the backup center. It was the beginning of the end of the Cavs' playoff run. "It was a highly competitive series, even after Chones got hurt," Carr said.

Then a student at Kent State, my college roommate and I scrounged up enough money to buy standing-room-only tickets to

Game 7 of the Bullets' semifinal series at the Coliseum. We went to the Plasma Alliance in Akron, sold some plasma for $20, had dinner at McDonald's, and still had enough money to buy tickets. We saw one of the greatest games in Cavs' history when Dick Snyder's shot over Phil Chenier toppled the mighty Bullets.

6 "I'm Coming Home"

It was a historic day in Cleveland. After weeks of speculation, LeBron James announced on July 11, 2014, that he was coming home. He picked *Sports Illustrated*'s website to tell the world.

It's a move that would have seemed unfathomable four years earlier, after the venomous fallout that followed his decision to leave Cleveland for the Miami Heat. "My relationship with Northeast Ohio is bigger than basketball," James told SI.com. "I didn't realize that four years ago. I do now."

The Cavaliers signed him to a two-year maximum deal, starting at $20.7 million in 2014–15. It had an out clause after the first season. The 6'8", 250-pound James turned the Cavs into an immediate contender. James shunned a press conference after the gigantic announcement—one of the biggest sports stories ever in Northeast Ohio.

He returned to the Cavs, where he spent the first seven years of his NBA career and helped them to the 2007 NBA Finals. James left the Cavs in July 2010 when he made the ill-fated *Decision* on ESPN. He broke the hearts of Cavs' fans everywhere when he said he was "taking his talents to South Beach." Fans reacted angrily to him leaving, as several burned his No. 23 Jersey.

"I was leaving something I had spent a long time creating," he told SI.com. "If I had to do it all over again, I'd obviously do things differently, but I'd still have left. I became a better player and a better man."

James helped the Heat to four NBA Finals appearances, which included championships in 2012 and 2013. James thanked Heat owner Micky Arison and team president Pat Riley for his four "amazing" years in Miami.

He said he only left the Cavs the first time because he was in search of titles. "When I left Cleveland, I was on a mission," he said. "I was seeking championships, and we won two. But Miami already knew that feeling. Our city hasn't had that feeling in a long, long, long time. But what's most important for me is bringing one trophy back to Northeast Ohio. I always believed that I'd return to Cleveland and finish my career there. I just didn't know when."

As stated previously, it was important to James and his wife, Savannah, to raise their family in the Akron area. They have three children, including two boys who are already quite accomplished on the basketball court. "I wasn't going to leave Miami for anywhere except Cleveland," he said. "The more time passed, the more it felt right. This is what makes me happy."

When he left in 2010, Cavs majority owner Dan Gilbert wrote a scathing letter ripping James. That was reportedly a major sticking point in James' decision, according to *ESPN The Magazine's* Chris Broussard. James said he's hashed out his differences with Gilbert. The Cavs owner said he flew to Miami to apologize to James during the free-agent period.

"I've met with Dan, face-to-face, man-to-man," James said. "We've talked it out. Everybody makes mistakes. I've made mistakes as well. Who am I to hold a grudge?"

The Cavs boast some of the best young talent in the league, which includes two-time All-Star Kyrie Irving, guard Dion Waiters, and No. 1 overall draft pick Andrew Wiggins. "I'm not promising a championship," James said. "I know how hard that is to deliver. We're not ready right now. My patience will get tested. I know that.

Gilbert Makes Nice with James

Rumors were rampant on July 6, 2014, that Cavs owner Dan Gilbert flew to Miami to meet with free agent LeBron James. It went viral on Twitter when the news was first reported by WKRK-92.3 FM's Joe Lull.

Gilbert tweeted that he was in his backyard enjoying the beautiful day.

If that were true, he must have broken all land speed records getting to the airport, where he hopped on his private jet and flew south. He admitted he flew to Miami to meet with James on that fateful Sunday, according to a story on Yahoo! Sports. It was vitally important to this entire story since most people thought Heat president Pat Riley was the only front-office executive who met face-to-face with James in the entire free-agent process. Obviously, that wasn't the case.

Gilbert had some fence-mending to do with James after writing the infamous letter in July 2010. "We had five great years together and one terrible night," Gilbert said he told James.

That started the reconciliation. "I told him how sorry I was, expressed regret for how that night went and how I let all the emotion and passion for the situation carry me away," he said. "I told him I wish I had never done it, that I wish I could take it back."

James quickly told Gilbert he regretted *The Decision*.

"It was more comfortable than I actually thought it would be," Gilbert said. "They made it easy for me."

I'm going into a situation with a young team and a new coach [in David Blatt]. But this is not about the roster or the organization. I feel my calling here goes above basketball. I have a responsibility to lead, in more ways than one, and I take that very seriously."

James is a 10-time All-Star and a four-time Most Valuable Player. He's averaged 27.1 points, 7.2 rebounds, and 6.9 assists in the first 11 seasons of his career. "I'm ready to accept the challenge," he said. "I'm coming home."

In his first season back in Cleveland, James wore many hats. He said that when the Cavaliers lose, he shoulders all the blame. However, when they win, it's a team victory. "Everything that goes on with this team falls on me," he said. "Everything. Wins, losses, popcorn, concessions, tickets, everything."

At that point, a reporter asked, "What about media credentials?"

"Yeah," James joked. "Did you get yours okay?"

Obviously, he was having some fun. However, he's taken "ownership" of this entire franchise from top to bottom, and that might not be a bad thing. He knows what it takes to win an NBA championship, and everyone is following his lead. He is showing the many facets of his game. He doesn't consider himself merely a small forward. "I don't have a position," he said. "I'm just a ballplayer. Put me out on the floor I'll make something happen. I've always tried to be a triple-threat: score, pass and defend, rebound, whatever the case may be to help my team win."

Warriors coach Steve Kerr said he wasn't surprised that James was worn down to start the 2014–2015 season. "He's been to the NBA Finals four straight years," he said. "It just absolutely saps the life out of you year after year. He's the focal point of everything in this league and with his team and the energy he expends on both ends of the floor. He wasn't himself to start the season, but how could he be after this four-year run? The fact that he's motoring on and playing at a high level speaks to his competitiveness and the fact that break probably helped him as much mentally as it did physically."

James admitted it is draining going to the Finals. "I would love to keep getting drained," he said. "I'll take it."

Of course, the Cavs advanced to the NBA Finals against Kerr's Warriors. James became the first NBA player since a group of Boston Celtics players in 1966 to make it to the Finals in five consecutive seasons.

7 The Shot

Los Angeles Lakers star Magic Johnson called the Cavs the NBA's Team of the '90s.

Despite that lofty praise from the Hall of Famer, they couldn't get past the Chicago Bulls in the playoffs. They were eliminated by the Bulls in the postseason in 1988, '89, '92, '93, and '94. That grief was largely because of one man—Michael Jordan—arguably the best player ever.

None of the losses hurt more than on May 7, 1989, in a 101–100 verdict in Game 5 of the Eastern Conference first-round playoff series before 20,273 at Richfield Coliseum. It will forever be known in Cleveland folklore as "The Shot."

Jordan's 18-foot jumper at the buzzer shot down the Cavs. The picture of Jordan hanging in the air out near the foul line will forever be ingrained in the minds of sports fans. Cavs swingman Craig Ehlo was assigned the difficult task of guarding Jordan on the play.

Just seconds before, Ehlo had taken the ball out of bounds near halfcourt, only to get the ball back from forward Larry Nance to score on a layup to give the Cavs a 100–99 lead with three seconds left.

Three seconds could feel like an eternity in the NBA, especially with Jordan on the court.

Jordan was double-teamed by Ehlo and Nance on the inbounds. Jordan received the inbounds pass from Brad Sellers, shook free from both defenders and put the finishing touches on a 44-point effort. Jordan seemed to levitate on the play. After his jumper hit nothing but net, he pumped his fist, as Ehlo crumbled to the court.

Dramatic Sports Moments

Cleveland sports fans have experienced more than their share of grief through the years since the Browns captured the 1964 NFL championship. Here are some of them:

Red Right 88—January 4, 1981, Cleveland Municipal Stadium, AFC Division playoff game, Oakland Raiders 14, Cleveland Browns 12.

Red Right 88 was a pass play in the Browns' playbook. The Browns advanced to Oakland's 13-yard line with 49 seconds to play. Place-kicker Don Cockroft had already missed two field goals and an extra point on the frigid day—4° Fahrenheit. Quarterback Brian Sipe's pass intended to Hall of Fame tight end Ozzie Newsome was picked off in the end zone by Raiders safety Mike Davis. The Raiders went on to win the Super Bowl.

The Drive—January 11, 1987, AFC Championship Game, Cleveland Municipal Stadium, Denver Broncos 23, Cleveland Browns 20 (overtime).

Broncos quarterback John Elway engineered a 15-play, 98-yard drive in 5:02 to tie the game. Wide receiver Mark Jackson caught Elway's five-yard touchdown pass with 37 seconds left in regulation to send the game into overtime. Place-kicker Rich Karlis' 33-yard field goal with 5:48 left in OT was the game-winner.

The Fumble—January 17, 1988, Mile High Stadium, AFC Championship Game, Denver Broncos 38, Cleveland Browns 33.

Browns running back Earnest Byner was stripped of the ball on his way to the end zone with less than a minute to play. Denver defensive back Jeremiah Castille stripped the ball and recovered the fumble at the 1-yard line. The Browns were trying to tie the score at 38 and send it into overtime. Denver took an intentional safety after Castille's big play.

The Shot—May 7, 1989, Richfield Coliseum, Eastern Conference first round, Game 5, Chicago Bulls 101, Cleveland Cavaliers 100.

Bulls guard Michael Jordan stunned the Cavs with a game-winning jumper as time ran out.

The Move—November 6, 1995.

Owner Art Modell announced he signed a deal to relocate the Browns to Baltimore for the 1996 season. The Browns were able to keep their history and were awarded an expansion team in 1999.

1997 World Series—Game 7, Sunday, October 26, 1997, at Pro Player Stadium, Florida Marlins 3, Cleveland Indians 2 (11 innings).

Indians closer Jose Mesa's blown save allowed the Marlins to score a run in the bottom of the ninth on Craig Counsell's sacrifice fly, which tied the score at 2. Mesa was two outs away from the Indians' first championship since 1948. Florida pushed across the winning run in the 11th off Tribe right-hander Charles Nagy.

The Decision—July 8, 2010.

Cavaliers forward LeBron James announced on national television he was "taking his talents to South Beach" and signed a free-agent deal with the Miami Heat.

The Cavs had recorded a 6–0 record against the Bulls during the regular season. The Cavs had won a franchise-record 57 games that season, finishing 10 games ahead of Chicago in the Central Division. None of that mattered in the first round of the playoffs, which the Bulls won, three games to two.

The locker room was sullen, but not downtrodden. "The [media] came in and were like, 'How gut-wrenching is this?'" Cavs center Brad Daugherty told the *Chicago Tribune*. "I was thinking, *This isn't gut-wrenching. We didn't play well enough to win and a guy who is a hell of a player made a hell of a play to beat us.*"

They weren't aware of the significance of what Jordan's shot would mean to his legacy. "Being in the first round, the magnitude didn't seem as great at the time," Cavs guard Mark Price told the *Tribune*. "It's grown over time."

Daugherty, arguably the best center in Cavs' history, said the players didn't dwell on the loss. "It was amazing to be part of that [rivalry]," Daugherty said. "I maybe would've won a ring or two [if not for the Bulls], but life goes on, and life is pretty good."

8 Cavs Return to the Finals

It was a long, winding road to the 2015 NBA Finals for the Cavaliers. They struggled mightily at one point in the season. It's difficult to fathom that the Cavs were 19–20 at one point during the 2014–2015 season before kicking it into high gear.

LeBron James missed eight games during the Cavs' bumpy start to the new year. He returned for the Phoenix game on January 13. The Cavs dipped under .500 with a 107–100 loss to the Suns.

From that point on in the regular season, they went 34–9.

Cavs general manager David Griffin orchestrated two major deals that reshaped the roster. First, he sent shooting guard Dion Waiters to the Oklahoma City Thunder in a three-team trade on January 5, 2015.

They acquired guards Iman Shumpert and J.R. Smith from the New York Knicks and a protected 2015 first-round pick from the Thunder. Two days later, he shipped two first-round picks to the Denver Nuggets for 7'1", 250-pound center Timofey Mozgov. The Cavaliers were desperate for a rim protector.

"We talk about fit," Griffin said. "I know it's not sexy, but Timofey fits. We need guys to do the [dirty] work. He's skilled in ways people don't understand. He can make a facing jump shot. He can protect the rim. He's a true center. A player of his value is biggest in the biggest games."

Griffin said the Cavaliers were successful in addressing three key weaknesses on their team: a consistent outside shooter (Smith), a defensive-minded wing defender (Shumpert), and a starting center with length that has a defensive identity (Mozgov).

"We can now battle with any size we face," Griffin said.

James said he thought the moves improved the team. "I know once Andy [Varejao] went down, we needed to get bigger in the interior," he said. "Adding a guy like this to protect the rim will protect our team as well. We'll see if those are three pieces that can help us. Until we all get healthy and get on the floor together, we won't know."

Waiters was a talented player, but he wasn't a perfect fit on the Cavs' roster. "Dion is a talented player with potential ahead of him," Griffin said. "Trades like this are always difficult to make because there are relationships and bonds built, and that was the case with Dion. At the same time, we're very excited to welcome Iman and J.R. to Cleveland. With their size and versatility, we think both Iman and J.R. can help our team on both ends of the court, and we look forward to them joining us."

The early struggles were a result of the team not playing together. It had potential, but not continuity. "[We] are talented, but new," then Cavs coach David Blatt said. "We have a lot of work to do before we start claiming anything. We're talking about being the best team we can be. We want to progress from day to day and put us in a position to compete with anyone. We have the personalities and the right kind of character guys to compete every night."

Everyone on the team realized how special the team could be.

"I'm excited for the city of Cleveland and the state of Ohio," Blatt said. "People are so enthused by this team and what we're trying to do. I'm sure it's going to be an exciting place to be and a very, very exuberant atmosphere."

Once the Cavs advanced to the postseason, they bulldozed their way through the playoffs. They swept both Boston in the first round and Atlanta in the Eastern Conference Finals. That set up a dream matchup with Golden State in the NBA Finals. The Cavs stormed to a 2–1 lead in the best-of-seven series when Warriors coach Steve

Kerr decided to insert small forward Andre Iguodala into the starting lineup in Game 4. It was a stroke of genius.

They decided they didn't want to pound away at the Cavs' bruising front line of Timofey Mozgov and Tristan Thompson. Listening to a suggestion from one of his little-known coaching assistants, Kerr spread the floor and attacked from the perimeter. The Cavs never recovered from Kerr's strategic move and lost the final three games of the series. Golden State won the series four games to two.

The Cavs lost power forward Kevin Love in the first round against Boston when his arm was pulled out of its socket by Celtics forward Kelly Olynyk. Thompson moved into the starting lineup and thrived in the postseason. They withstood that injury. When point guard Kyrie Irving fractured his kneecap in Game 1 of the NBA Finals, they couldn't survive, especially against a team as talented as the Warriors.

Irving walked to the team bus on crutches, an indication that the end was near for the Cavs. James, though, didn't allow the Cavs to go down easily. He put up some staggering numbers. He was one assist shy of his fourth triple-double in the series in Game 6. In those six games, he averaged 35.8 points, 13.3 rebounds, and 8.8 assists in 45.8 minutes a game. He recorded three games of 40 or more points, not to mention a 39-point effort.

He said he believed the Cavs could win the series until time ran off the clock in the sixth game. "Yeah, when the numbers went to zero and we lost tonight, that's when I doubted," James said. "That's when it was over.

"I mean, I obviously knew it was going to be a tough task, and I continued to tell you guys we were undermanned. I don't know any other team—and I've been watching basketball for a long time; I'm a historian of the game—that's gotten to the Finals without two All-Stars. I cannot even remember thinking of it. I don't know if it's ever happened."

2015 NBA Finals
Game 1 — June 4 (at Golden State): Warriors 108, Cavs 100
Game 2 — June 7 (at Golden State): Cavs 95, Warriors 93
Game 3 — June 9 (at Cleveland): Cavs 96, Golden State 91
Game 4 — June 11 (at Cleveland): Warriors 103, Cavs 82
Game 5 — June 14 (at Golden State): Warriors 104, Cavs 91
Game 6 — June 16 (at Cleveland): Warriors 105, Cavs 97
(Warriors win series 4–2)

Love and Irving were obviously missed. They also were without Varejao, who ruptured his Achilles' tendon in late December. "[We] tried as much as we could to make up for those guys, but that's a lot of talent sitting in suits," James said. "I've had a lot of playoff runs, been on both ends, and I know one thing, that you've got to be healthy. You've also got to be playing great at the right time. You've got to have a little luck. And we were playing great, but we had no luck and we weren't healthy."

It doesn't get any easier losing in the Finals. He's experienced two losses in the Finals in Cleveland and Miami in addition to his two championships with the Heat. "All four of them are disappointing," he said. "It's not one higher or lower or in the middle. You don't win, it's disappointing. [It] doesn't matter if I'm playing in Miami or playing in Cleveland or playing on Mars. You lose the Finals, it's disappointing."

9 The Turbulent & Triumphant 2015–2016 Season

Obviously, any team with LeBron James on the roster is going to be very good. The Cavaliers ended the 2014–2015 season in the NBA Finals with a depleted roster. Three of their mainstays—All-Star guard Kyrie Irving, power forward Kevin Love, and valuable big man Anderson Varejao—were on the sideline in expensive suits.

When the highly anticipated 2015–2016 season opened, there was more uncertainty. The Cavs didn't have their full arsenal of weapons put together by the front office with the league's highest payroll of $108 million. Irving fractured his left kneecap in Game 1 of the 2015 NBA Finals against Golden State. Off-season surgery sidelined him for more than seven months. He missed the entire preseason and the first 24 games of the regular season before finally making his season debut against Philadelphia on December 20, 2015. Irving appeared in 53 games during his sometimes rocky regular season.

The Cavs started the season 17–7 without Irving in the lineup. Matthew Dellavedova and Mo Williams played the bulk of the minutes at point guard. The Cavs wanted to make sure Irving was 100 percent before he returned to the court. "I've been ready to play, but biomechanically, we just wanted to make sure everything was good so I'm not putting myself at higher risk to go out there and get hurt again," he told the Associated Press.

Irving credited the Cavs' medical team for getting him acclimated for NBA action. "Our staff did an unbelievable job of getting me prepared, going through the long rigorous months of kind of being down and out, getting hurt in Game 1 of the Finals and now, here we are, almost six, going on seven months, and now I'm back and ready to play," he said. "You wouldn't wish injury on anybody, just going through those months, just being a prisoner of your own emotions and thoughts. That's the hardest thing. Getting yourself out of [that funk] and thinking about what's the goal and task that's important to you. Life will hit you with a whole bunch of punches at once, and you gotta withstand it. You've got to persevere, and I'm glad that I'm at this point."

Irving was far from the only injured player at the start of the season. Four other key players were also recovering from injuries.

Love suffered a dislocated left shoulder in Game 4 of the 2015 first-round playoff series against Boston. He vowed to be back for the start of the 2015–2016 season, and he was in the starting lineup in the season opener at Chicago.

Varejao missed much of the 2014–2015 season and all of the postseason with a torn Achilles' tendon. He worked hard to get back for the start of the 2015–2016 season but wasn't around for the end of it—at least not with the Cavs. Fan favorite Varejao was dealt to Portland in a three-team trade at the deadline in February. The Cavs acquired valuable three-point shooter Channing Frye from the Orlando Magic in the deal. Varejao played the first 12 years of his career in Cleveland. He was immediately waived by Portland and signed as a free agent with Golden State.

Cavs center Timofey Mozgov had off-season knee surgery and was also in the lineup on opening night against the Bulls. However, he didn't come back the same intimidating rim protector he was during the Cavs' run to the Finals in 2015. Some thought he might have come back too soon. He lost his starting job to Tristan Thompson midway through the season. By the time the playoffs rolled around, he rarely got off the bench. Mozgov, an unrestricted free agent in the summer of 2016, might have cost himself millions of dollars on the open market.

Guard Iman Shumpert suffered a wrist injury before training camp started, which led to surgery on September 30, 2015. The defensive specialist missed the first 21 regular-season games. He made his season debut at Orlando on December 11, 2015. He appeared in 54 games during the season.

Not only were there medical concerns, the Cavs made a bold coaching change in January when David Blatt was fired and replaced by lead assistant Tyronn Lue. Through all the drama, the Cavs finished with the top record in the Eastern Conference at 57–25. The 57 wins tied for third on the Cavs' all-time list.

Cavs point guard Kyrie Irving missed the first 24 games of the 2015–2016 season and then struggled to find his game before finding it in a big way during the NBA Finals against the Golden State Warriors.

It was anything but easy for Irving, who averaged 19.6 points and posted career lows in assists (4.7) and three-point shooting (32.1 percent). He reflected on what was a fairly difficult regular season for him. "It wasn't pretty, personally, just because of the mental stress that was put on from going from June 4, when I got injured, to going through months and months of rehab to figuring out how to walk again, figuring out how to jump, figuring out how to run," he told the *Medina County Gazette*. "All those steps I had to go through, I haven't forgotten. It kind of carried over to the court. I just had to figure out how to be pretty good at the game again."

Lue said his star point guard has grown as a player. "This injury really helped him mature as far as taking care of his body, eating right, lifting weights, doing whatever you need to maintain your body," he said. "He understands with the long, grueling seasons like we had last year and the team we have now, we could play into June every year."

Of course, Lue has also come into his own as a rookie head coach. At age 39, he's not much older than some of his veterans. "I treat the guys like men," he said. "I played the game before. If you treat them like men and tell them the truth, they can respect you. They know what's at stake. They know what our goal was since the beginning of the season."

Cavs owner Dan Gilbert has been reluctant to speak about the coaching change. "I just think it was a great decision that was made," Gilbert told cleveland.com. "You never know what would happen any other way, but I think [Lue is] fantastic. It's rare that a guy knows the game and has people skills. You get both with him, like offense and defense almost. He's a special guy."

The Reign Man

The *Sports Illustrated* issue hit the newsstands on May 4, 1998, with the blaring headline, "Where's Daddy?" The investigative piece uncovered the fact that Cavaliers forward Shawn Kemp had fathered seven out-of-wedlock children with six different women. Written by Grant Wahl and L. Jon Wertheim, it was a major scoop for the weekly publication.

Cleveland-area reporters converged on Cavs' practice at Gund Arena and requested to speak to Kemp. Cavaliers PR man Bob Zink huddled the media together and informed reporters, "If you ask about the *Sports Illustrated* story, I'm going to end the interview."

Everyone grumbled. This was a big, national story. Reporters had to ask about it.

Kemp came out to face the music. He was always very good to deal with and extremely media-friendly. The *Akron Beacon Journal's* Chris Tomasson asked the first question.

"Can you tell us about the *Sports Illustrated* story?" Tomasson asked.

"That's it," Zink said, waving his arms and ending the interview. "We're done."

That was the end of that day's interview. The media eventually talked to Kemp about the "scandal," but not that day. Kemp earned millions of dollars during his 14-year NBA career. A large percentage of it went to child support.

The Cavs traded their two best players—point guard Terrell Brandon and power forward Tyrone Hill—to the Milwaukee Bucks in a three-team deal with Seattle on September 25, 1997. The Cavs acquired Kemp, one of the league's high-flying dunking machines. The Bucks sent Vin Baker to the SuperSonics. The Cavs immediately struck a long-term deal with Kemp worth $107 million over seven years. They finally landed their superstar.

Interest in the team had waned in recent years after the end of the Brad Daugherty–Mark Price–Larry Lance era. Ownership felt the Cavs needed star power to revitalize interest in the team that had moved downtown to Gund Arena. The blockbuster trade resulted in one first-round playoff appearance. The Cavs lost in the 1998 playoffs to the Indiana Pacers, three games to one. Kemp averaged 26 points and 10.3 rebounds in the series, but was unable to get past the talented Pacers. Indiana had too much firepower with Reggie Miller, Mark Jackson, and Detlef Schrempf.

Kemp made his sixth—and final—All-Star appearance in 1998. He also became the first Cavs player to start for the Eastern Conference team. He would never reach those heights as a player again. He showed up at training camp the following year at 315 pounds. In my report on the annual Wine & Gold Scrimmage at Gund Arena, I said it looked like he was dragging a refrigerator up and down the court.

Rumors surfaced that Kemp might be abusing drugs and alcohol. He lasted three seasons in Cleveland. General manager Jim Paxson traded him to Portland on August 30, 2000. Kemp's career ended three years later in Orlando during the 2002–2003 season.

11 Carlos Boozer's Escape

The Cavaliers made an astute pick when they selected Duke forward/center Carlos Boozer in the second round of the 2002 draft. He was the 34th overall selection but played like a lottery pick. He

"See You Next Tuesday"

Carlos Boozer was set to make his first return to Gund Arena after spurning the Cavs in free agency the previous summer. Boozer's underhanded exit from Cleveland was a huge controversy the previous July.

The Utah Jazz made their only appearance in Cleveland on March 15, 2005. Cavs coach Paul Silas was asked about Boozer's return during practice the day before the game. He didn't have much to say about it, but while chatting after the media session, Silas brought up Boozer and said, "See you next Tuesday." I had no idea what he was talking about.

Of course, upon further review, if you replaced "see you" with "C U," the acronym spelled a word that wasn't very complimentary of the star power forward. One other media member was included in the conversation, Mike Snyder, the host of the Cavs' pregame show on WTAM, the team's flagship radio station.

Somehow, nationally syndicated radio host Jim Rome got his hands on the sound byte and played it several times the next day. Silas was fined $10,000 by the team for making the inappropriate comment.

Boozer didn't even suit up for the much-to-do-about-nothing game. He sat out with an injury.

The next day on March 16, I flew to Milwaukee. I took a cab to my hotel, the Downtown Courtyard by Marriott, and settled in for an afternoon nap. The phone rang, which startled me awake from a great siesta.

Cavs vice president of communications Ted Carper was furious. He accused me of furnishing Rome with the Silas recording from practice. I assured him that I had not even recorded the post-media session.

It turned out that WTAM had inadvertently sent the recording over a network that was intercepted by Rome's staff.

played two seasons for the Cavs and was one of the league's most underpaid performers in 2003–2004 when he averaged 15.5 points and 11.4 rebounds.

The Cavs owned a team option worth $695,000 on Boozer's 2004–2005 contract. It was quite obvious he was worth almost 10 times that amount. Cavs owner Gordon Gund and general manager Jim Paxson worked out an apparent wink-wink deal with Boozer and his agent, Rob Pelinka. The Cavs wouldn't pick up the option on his deal, making him a restricted free agent. Boozer reportedly agreed to re-sign with the Cavs for their full mid-level exception of $40 million for six years. But once he became a free agent, Pelinka started negotiating with other teams. He signed a six-year, $68 million deal with Utah on July 14, 2004.

The Cavs were crestfallen. They had put their trust in Boozer, whom they had planned on building around. He would have comprised a frontcourt that included center Zydrunas Ilgauskas and small forward LeBron James. The Cavs thought it had championship DNA. Instead, it all came crashing down like a house of cards.

"I decided to trust Carlos and show him the respect he asked for," Gund said. "He did not show that trust and respect in return. That's what happened." Boozer disputed the Cavs' claim that he agreed to a long-term deal with the team. He said the Cavs questioned his reputation and character by alleging he backed out of a promise.

Many believe Boozer and his agent got greedy. They front-loaded the first year of the contract with the Jazz knowing the Cavs couldn't afford to pay him the $11 million. The Cavs were situated about $4 million under the salary cap. They would have had to cut several hefty contracts to carve out $11 million. Gund admitted later he wouldn't have matched the offer under any circumstances. He no longer wanted Boozer on his team. When Boozer broke his word to Gund, that forever damaged his relationship with the player. Gund was a shrewd businessman, but very honorable.

Many thought the Boozer fiasco set the franchise back a couple of years. Paxson recovered a bit by acquiring two young power forwards from Orlando in exchange for Tony Battie and some draft picks. Those two youngsters were Drew Gooden and Anderson Varejao.

However, Boozer's name will forever be mud in Cleveland.

12 LeBron James' Debut

LeBron James, the No. 1 pick in the 2003 NBA Draft, had taken the league by storm. He had just finished a so-so preseason when he shot just 34 percent from the field. That did nothing to thwart the media from showing up in full force for the Cavs' 2003–2004 regular-season opener in Sacramento on October 29.

Arco Arena was buzzing with excitement. Kings owner Joe Maloof couldn't stop thanking the NBA for granting his franchise the chance to host James in such a big event. Dignitaries and celebrities showed up for James' first game, a theme that would continue throughout his career. The media had surmised that the 18-year-old James might average around 15 or 16 points during his rookie year. Coach Paul Silas elevated the rookie into the starting lineup at point guard.

The Kings issued an astounding 350 media credentials—about twice as many as they would for a normal game. That kind of attention might equate to a second-round playoff game, Kings director of media relations Troy Hanson said. The NBA had better get used to that almost overbearing attention on the Chosen One. Welcome to LeBron's world. It had been going on since he was in high school.

Normally for the Cleveland-area media covering the team, there would be five to 10 reporters for pregame media availability. Just a few months since he graduated from St. Vincent–St. Mary High School in Akron, James' pregame availability outside the Cavs' locker room that night drew about a hundred media members. Things would never be the same for the Cavs or James' teammates. Some of the other players on the team bristled at all the congestion and foot traffic in and around the locker room.

LeBron James makes a no-look pass during his NBA debut with the Cavs against the Kings in Sacramento on October 29, 2003.

Once the nationally televised game began, James put on a dazzling performance. He finished with 25 points, six rebounds, nine assists, and four steals in the Cavs' 106–92 loss. Evidently, the first-year player was going to be much better than advertised. Such was the case for one of the NBA's all-time greats. "I think that was LeBron's statement to the league that he's here," James' agent, Aaron Goodwin, told ESPN. "He's for real."

James couldn't believe the attention he was generating. "It's kind of crazy," James told the *Cleveland Plain Dealer*. "Now I'm finally here. It's a dream. I'd be here until after the game if I really talked about how happy I am to be here."

Silas recognized early on what a special player he was now coaching. Fundamentally, he was as good as any player on the team. "When we first entered the arena nobody knew exactly what LeBron was going to do," Silas said. "I thought he was going to be good, but not nearly as good as he was. It was unbelievable."

The Cavs thought they had something special team-wise with a starting lineup that included 7'3" center Zydrunas Ilgauskas, power forward Carlos Boozer, small forward Darius Miles, shooting guard Ricky Davis, and James.

It was athletic, potent offensively, and had elite size. That euphoria didn't last long, however. A rumor circulated that Davis had a run-in with James in Portland on the road trip. General manager Jim Paxson wasted little time before shipping him off to Boston. Remember, it was now all about James. The team would try to appease him at every turn, and that meant putting the right players around him.

James was asked if the overbearing attention was starting to get old. "Once it gets old," he said, "I'll stop playing."

13 Cavs Draft Austin Carr in 1971

Austin Carr was sitting in art history class at Notre Dame at South Bend, Indiana, when word finally reached him that he was the first overall pick in the 1971 NBA Draft by the Cavaliers. Of course, ESPN was just a figment of someone's imagination at the time. The same could be said of social media. News didn't travel at lightning speed as it does now. So it was during a break in class when the 6′4″, 200-pound Carr was told that he had been drafted No. 1. After a couple of slaps on the back, class resumed.

"It wasn't like it is now," Carr said. "Today, they bring you to New York and buy you a new suit. It wasn't marketed that way 40 years ago."

Carr was one of the leading scorers in the nation for the Fighting Irish, but never won an NCAA scoring title. He averaged 38

Austin Carr, flanked by Cavs coach Bill Fitch (left) and team owner Nick Mileti, announces his signing with the Cavs at a press conference on April 5, 1971. The Cavs selected the All-America guard out of Notre Dame with the No. 1 overall pick in the NBA Draft.

points per game as a senior in 1970–1971, but finished second to Mississippi forward Johnny Neumann's 40.1. Carr also had to deal with LSU's prolific Pete Maravich earlier in his career. "Pistol Pete" won three consecutive NCAA scoring titles and averaged a record-setting 44.2 points per game in his career.

Carr averaged a school-record 34.6 points per game in his three years at Notre Dame. He was a two-time All-American and the 1971 Naismith College Player of the Year. After Cavs coach Bill Fitch landed on Carr, he knew he had selected a major talent. "We felt we had to have someone of superstar status," Fitch told the *Cleveland Plain Dealer*. "I think he can be a superstar in his first year. He fits into our plans for next season of running and shooting."

The Cavs won a coin toss with Portland to win the first pick in the draft. At the time, the teams with the worst records in each conference participated in a coin toss for the top pick. That was the beginning of the NBA Draft lottery that exists today. The Cavs also accepted $25,000 from the Trail Blazers for a promise to not pick UCLA forward Sidney Wicks with the top pick. Still, there were rumors that the Cavs would take Kentucky State center Elmore Smith, who would later play for the team.

"It was nowhere near as sophisticated as it is now," Carr said in an interview with the Sports Research Center. "It wasn't the big, celebrity-filled thing that it is now."

The Cavs thought they had landed a cornerstone piece, a player they would build around. Carr still holds the NCAA tournament record with his 61-point outburst against Ohio University in 1971. His 41.3-point average in NCAA tournament games might never be touched.

Unfortunately, throughout his NBA career, injuries played a major role. Carr suffered a stress fracture to the fifth metatarsal in his right foot in training camp on September 14, 1971. He missed the first month of the season. "As far as I'm concerned it is [one of the biggest disappointments of my career] because I was really looking forward to starting the season out," he told reporters after the injury. "Now I stand to miss about 15 games."

He still averaged 21.2 points in 43 games during his first season with the Cavs and earned a spot on the All-Rookie Team. "I was playing well," Carr said. "I just couldn't stay healthy. I would have liked to see how I played without the injuries."

So would longtime followers of the team. He wasn't in LeBron James' all-world class, but Carr would have been right behind him in the franchise's pecking order. As it stands, Carr is fourth on the team's all-time list in scoring behind James, Zydrunas Ilgauskas, and Brad Daugherty. "I would have scored at least 20,000 points," Carr said.

After breaking a bone in his right foot, he suffered an injury to his right knee. "The right side was my nemesis," Carr said. He finally visited a group of doctors in Los Angeles who he said straightened it out. "I played four or five seasons without any problems," he said.

Carr and Lenny Wilkens made up the starting backcourt for the Cavs in the 1972–1973 and 1973–1974 seasons. That first season together, they both averaged more than 20 points a game—a rare occurrence in those days. "Now, that happens all the time," Carr said. "Back then, we were one of the first to do that."

Carr said he learned so much playing with Wilkens. "When I came into the league, I was a true two-guard," Carr said. "I didn't know anything about playmaking. I never had to do it. Scoring was my game. Lenny taught me to be a true combo guard. If it wasn't for him, I would have had trouble with longevity. He taught me so much about the game. He taught me a different vision."

Analysts always talk about players being like a coach on the court. "That's exactly what Lenny was," Carr said. "Because of my injury situation, I learned how to survive in this league being a step slower. I attribute that to him."

The feeling was mutual for Wilkens. "I loved playing with [Carr]," he said. "I hope I influenced him in some way."

14 Fitch Throws a Chair

Long before Indiana University men's basketball coach Bob Knight threw a chair onto the court, Cavs coach Bill Fitch cornered the market on outlandish displays of temper.

He was upset with a call made by official Bob Rakel and tossed a metal folding chair onto the court on October 29, 1971, in a 98–97 loss to Atlanta in Cleveland Arena. The *Cleveland Press'* Paul Tepley, one of the country's quintessential sports photographers, was the only shooter to capture the historic picture. It's still making its rounds to this day. Fitch was fined $3,000 by the NBA, an exorbitant figure in that era. If it had happened in today's NBA, he'd be suspended for half the season. The Hall of Fame coach, always the king of one-liners, said he was also fined by Cavs owner Nick Mileti. "He fined me $100 for missing [the ref]," he told ESPN's Bill Simmons.

Phoenix Suns coach Cotton Fitzsimmons might have had the best line about Fitch's antics. "Thank God you weren't sitting on a couch," he said.

Fitch was quick with the one-liners. It was all done for a reason. "He was a very smart guy," *Cleveland Plain Dealer* and *Press* beat writer Burt Graeff said. "He would try to cover up with all that crazy stuff to deflect all the losses."

Point guard Lenny Wilkens said he loved playing two seasons for Fitch. "He was an interesting guy," Wilkens said. "He just wanted to win. He was all about the fundamentals. We were always prepared." Wilkens said he used to sit with Fitch after practice and just talk about the nuances of the game. "The other players said I was a POW—a prisoner of war," Wilkens joked.

Fitch could be extremely hard on his players. Wilkens said he had a great relationship with him. "When I stepped on the floor, I was ready to play," he said.

Cavs guard Austin Carr called Fitch a task-master. "I had a high school coach just like that," he said. "I understood what he was all about. He was tough. He made us tougher." One preseason, Carr said they didn't play any games. "[Fitch] had practice for 30 straight days," he said. "That's how it was back then."

15 Joe Tait Broadcasts Last Game

It was a sad and retrospective day at Quicken Loans Arena on April 13, 2011. Joe Tait, the radio voice of the Cavs, was calling it quits after 39 years with the team. He started calling their games during the Cavs' inaugural season in 1970.

Tait called almost 3,100 games with the Cavs, never working on the radio with an analyst. He viewed the analyst as a burden. A two-man booth worked perfectly well for others, but for him, he felt he didn't need one. His broadcast location in Section 126 at Quicken Loans Arena will forever be known as the "Joe Tait Perch." He won the Curt Gowdy Media Award in May 2010. It's given every year by the Naismith Memorial Basketball Hall of Fame to basketball writers and broadcasters.

Tait was hospitalized with pneumonia in the 2010 preseason. Testing showed he needed heart surgery, which caused him to miss almost the entire 2010–2011 season. He was replaced by WTAM-AM 1100's Mike Snyder and Jim Chones. Tait returned on March 25, 2011, for a handful of home games. The Cavs honored him with Joe Tait Appreciation Night on April 8, 2011, in a game against the Chicago Bulls. They raised a commemorative banner to the rafters. Instead of retiring his number, his banner was adorned with a microphone, and listed his years of service to the team (1970–1981, 1983–2011). As a tribute, I encouraged the local media to wear their favorite "Tait sweaters" that night. Many of them did, including television broadcasters Fred McLeod and Austin Carr.

During Tait's two-year hiatus, he covered the New Jersey Nets on the radio in 1981–1982, and the Chicago Bulls on television in 1982–1983. Paul Porter replaced Tait in the broadcast booth on WBBG in Cleveland those two years.

As Tait's broadcasting career with the Cavs came to an end, it was a sad time for many fans. As his final game against Washington was coming to a close, Frank Sinatra's "My Way" played throughout the arena. In-house cameras focused on Tait sitting in his perch. It brought tears to the eyes of many in the crowd and watching the game on television. Tait normally closed his broadcast with, "Have a good night, everybody!" On this night, his last, he ended with, "This is Joe Tait...have a good life, everybody!"

He was replaced by play-by-play man John Michael and analyst Chones for the 2011–2012 season.

Unbeknownst to many fans, Tait was not the original voice of the Cavs in their inaugural season. That distinction belongs to Bob Brown, who broadcast the first 11 games on WERE radio during the 1970–1971 season. He was also the team's public-relations director. Tait's first game was at Cleveland Arena against the Milwaukee Bucks on November 4, 1970. Bucks center Lew Alcindor scored 53 points in Milwaukee's 110–108 victory. The Cavs dropped to 0–12. They started the season with 15 consecutive losses.

A native of Evanston, Illinois, Tait, who was 33 at the time, had been program director at WBOW in Terre Haute, Indiana, and was doing play-by-play for the Indiana Hoosiers men's basketball team. Dick McCauley, general manager at WERE, said he was grateful for Brown to start the season with the Cavs. "We believe Tait will keep

---

Memorable Tait One-Liners

Radio broadcaster Joe Tait, the voice of the Cavaliers, was always quick with the wit. Here are some of his signature calls:

"It's basketball time at The Q" — *his sign-on for home games*
"Wham with the right hand!" — *after a Cavs dunk*
"Three-ball" — *a three-point shot*
"Have a good night, everybody" — *how he ended each broadcast*

---

up the high quality of Cavaliers broadcasts," McCauley told the *Cleveland Plain Dealer* on October 31, 1970.

Cavs owner Nick Mileti said Brown did a fine job on the radio. "He's also the best in his field in public relations, and I need him in that job," he said. "Tait will do just fine. He's a pro."

Tait would be the team's radio voice for 39 years.

16 Kevin Love Gets Arm Torn out of Socket

Since entering the NBA in 2008, Kevin Love has dreamed of competing in the NBA playoffs. The power forward finally got his chance in Cleveland in 2015. Unfortunately, his playoff run lasted all of four games. Love dislocated his left shoulder in Game 4 of the first-round playoff series against Boston on April 26, 2015.

The circumstances of the injury were controversial. Celtics center Kelly Olynyk grabbed Love's left arm and pulled it out of the socket while competing for a rebound in the first quarter of the Cavs' 101–93 victory. Love grabbed his shoulder, ran off the court and into the TD Garden locker room. His season ended on the play, and he was not a happy camper afterward.

"I thought it was a bush-league play," Love told reporters after the game. "Olynyk was in a compromising position, had no chance to get the ball, and it's just too bad that he would go to those lengths to take somebody out of the game and do that to someone. I have no doubt in my mind that he did that on purpose."

The 6'10", 243-pound Love had surgery on his shoulder a few days later in New York and was scheduled to miss four to six months. He was ready for the start of the 2015–2016 season. Olynyk was called for a personal foul on the play. The NBA later suspended him for the first game of the 2015–2016 season. He told the *Boston Herald* there was no intention on his part to severely injure Love on the play. "That's ridiculous," Olynyk said. "I would never intentionally hurt Kevin or anyone else. I wish him a very speedy recovery."

Love said Olynyk's intent was clear. "That's just not a basketball play," Love said. "You look at the replay. Yeah, expect it to be physical, but when it has to go to that length, that's not the way it's supposed to be. That's not how you play basketball."

It proved to be another footnote in Cleveland's long-suffering sports history. With Love sidelined, along with the loss of Kyrie Irving in Game 1, the Cavs just didn't have the firepower to upend Golden State in the NBA Finals. The Cavaliers did get some encouraging news on the first day of free agency on July 1, 2015. Love proved to be a man of his word. The three-time All-Star power forward ended much speculation by agreeing to a five-year, $110 million contract with the Cavaliers. "I'm going back to Cleveland," he announced on the *Players' Tribune* website.

Love, an unrestricted free agent, opted out of his contract worth $16.7 million for the 2015–2016 season. The 26-year-old stated his desire to remain with the Cavaliers several times since the end of the regular season. Problem was, no one in the national media seemed to believe him. Once free agency kicked off July 1, the Cavaliers offered him a full maximum deal.

Rumors surfaced that Love was going to meet with the Los Angeles Lakers. Of course, that proved to be nothing but a myth.

"After Game 1 of the NBA Finals, that's when it really struck me," Love wrote on *Players' Tribune*. "Sitting on the sidelines, I never wanted to play in a game more than that one. I had dreamed of playing in the NBA Finals and I just wanted to help my guys win. I couldn't have been prouder of them as they poured their blood, sweat, and tears onto the court. Yeah, of course, I've heard the free agency rumors. But at the end of the day, and after meeting with my teammates (it turns out pools are great meeting places) and with the front office, it was clear Cleveland was the place for me. We're all on the same page and we're all in. We have unfinished business, and now it's time to get back to work."

Love averaged 16.4 points, 9.7 rebounds, and 2.2 assists in 75 games in his first season with the Cavs. He said he was looking for three main ingredients from prospective teams in free agency: happiness, the ability to win, and make a lot of money. Love was able to check all three boxes with the Cavaliers. "I'd already gone through the [recruiting] process in my head," he said on Sirius XM radio. "For me, I wanted to hash out everything on my own and follow my heart. I always felt Cleveland came out on top."

Love said LeBron James played a big role in his decision. When James and Love were spotted in a poolside cabana in Los Angeles on June 30, that meeting had a bearing on Love's decision. "There were several things that went into my decision-making process," Love said. "I did want to meet with LeBron and lay everything out on the table. It just so happened, we were both in L.A. at the same time. We laid it all out there, hung out, and had a leisurely conversation. We ended up in the same place."

The three-time All-Star said he's on the same page with James. "We're ready to go," Love said. "It will take a lot of work. You have to have luck and not be bit by the injury bug. It's the hardest thing in the world to get to the mountaintop. We'll continue to work for something special in Cleveland."

Love bristles when he's described as a "stretch-four." He's said he's a post player, who can shoot from the perimeter. In the 25-point win over Brooklyn on March 18, 2015, Love spent more time than usual operating in the post. "I wanted to be around the basket more," he said. "More than anything, it was running the floor and trying to catch the ball in the paint. I think I can get more touches down there. In the halfcourt, it's whatever comes my way."

Cavaliers coach David Blatt said Love being around the basket is not a foreign concept. "At different times this season, Kevin has played well in the post," he said. "It's not like it didn't exist before. Overall, his production has been great for us. His focus is helping us win games, regardless of his numbers."

Scoring points hadn't been a problem for the Cavaliers, who were sixth in the NBA in points scored during the 2014–2015 season. But Love alternated from looking lost in the offense to being a huge asset in what the Cavaliers were doing. Love said a balance needed to be found between his looks in the post and at the three-point line. "I learned early on, 'Go where they ain't, and try to space the floor,'" he said. "Try to mix it up. I'll try to find a good balance. It's something that can help us. Teams will try to take away different options on the team. It's got to be the next man stepping up, whether it's me or someone else. I feel comfortable."

17 Zydrunas Ilgauskas' Number Retirement

He was the Cavs' beloved giant. Zydrunas Ilgauskas spent 14 seasons with Cleveland after being a first-round pick in 1996. Ilgauskas had his No. 11 jersey retired on March 8, 2014, at Quicken Loans Arena.

Zydrunas Ilgauskas waves to the fans at Quicken Loans Arena during his number retirement ceremony on March 8, 2014. Ilgauskas played 12 seasons for the Cavs and is the team's all-time leader in rebounds, games played, and blocks, and is second only to LeBron James in points.

Stars poured out to honor Big Z, including Miami Heat forward LeBron James, who had the day off. His appearance fueled speculation that James might return to Cleveland when he became a free agent four months later. Of course, that's exactly what happened.

The Cavs chose the date after consulting with James, ESPN reported. James came to the gala event at Ilgauskas' request, but the process of picking the game revolved around the former's schedule and was orchestrated by the Cavs. James had hinted that he might consider returning to the team under the right circumstances. Ilgauskas' ceremony might have helped grease the skids for him to come back.

The 7′3″ Ilgauskas and James were teammates in Cleveland for seven years, as well as one in Miami. They remain very close off the court. "[LeBron] being here is an added bonus for me because of what we've been through together," Ilgauskas said. "I consider him a good friend. We played so much, achieved so much, failed many times, but also were successful a lot of times. For me, it would've been almost a distraction if he wasn't here. That he was able to witness that makes it that much more special.

"[Ex-Cavs general manager] Danny Ferry came to me and said, 'You know, you're the only person that can bring this group together in one room. Nobody else could.' I felt like those people touched my life so much more than I have theirs, so it was just special for them to take time out of their busy schedules and come to this occasion."

The ceremony totally overshadowed that night's game, won by the New York Knicks, 107–97. Ilgauskas' jersey was the seventh retired by the Cavs. He joined Austin Carr (34), Nate Thurmond (42), Bobby "Bingo" Smith (7), Larry Nance (22), Brad Daugherty (43), and Mark Price (25) in having their numbers raised to the rafters of Quicken Loans Arena. Radio broadcaster Joe Tait has also been honored by the team.

"When they look at that jersey, it's going to represent integrity and character, No. 1," Cavs owner Dan Gilbert said. "It's going to represent hard work, a lunch-pail, get-the-job-done kind of effort. It's going to represent the concept of never, ever, ever, ever giving up. Ever."

Ilgauskas overcame career-threatening foot injuries, which caused him to miss the entire 1996–1997 and 1999–2000 seasons, to become a two-time NBA All-Star. He was also the Cavs' franchise leader in rebounds, games played, and blocks. He's second on the all-time scoring list, trailing only James. "You guys [the fans] have been the main reason I kept getting back up after all the injuries and kept trying again," he said. "I loved coming here to work every day, no matter what our record was, and I miss that feeling of running out of that tunnel on this court every single day of my life. I love being part of this community. I love being part of this city. I just hope that you feel the same way about me. Thank you again for this incredible honor, and thank you again for giving me a place I can proudly call home."

He was surrounded by his family, wife Jennifer and sons Deividas and Povilas. They were adopted from an orphanage in Lithuania.

18 Mark Price: The Choir Boy

Mark Price might have had choir-boy looks, but he had the competitive fire of an assassin—a baby-faced assassin. Price was a devout Christian. Don't misinterpret that as being soft. Once he stepped onto the court, he was quite the competitor.

The Cavs' front office has been adept at finding good point guards over the years. Kevin Johnson, Terrell Brandon, and later Kyrie Irving—All-Star-quality talent—were all acquired by the Cavs through the draft. But their run of good luck started on June 17, 1986, when they sent a 1989 second-round pick and $50,000 to the Dallas Mavericks for Mark Price. Despite being the ACC's Most Valuable Player for the 1984–1985 season and having his college jersey retired, Price wasn't rated highly in the 1986 draft. Critics said he was too slow (not true), too small (he was about 6', 180 pounds), and not a superior athlete (totally false).

Once he came to training camp, Price immediately showed the Cavs he was ready for prime time. His development helped the Cavs transform into an Eastern Conference power. Price became one of the league's top shooters. He was also a lot tougher than anyone realized, and became a fan favorite. People identified with the deadly shooter, who went right after some of the best players in the league.

Price was also known as one of the league's best free-throw shooters. Future Hall of Famer Steve Nash nudged past Price on the NBA's all-time list in free-throw percentage. Nash finished his

Mark Price brings the ball upcourt against the Miami Heat in 1993. He held the Cavs record for career assists until LeBron James passed him in 2015.

career at 90.43 percent, a smidgen better than Price's 90.39 percent. Price became the first Cavs player to earn first-team All-NBA honors after the 1992–1993 season.

He was also adept at splitting double teams. "Mark really revolutionized the way that people attack the screen-and-roll," former Cavs teammate Steve Kerr told reporters. "To me, he was the first guy in the NBA who really split the screen-and-roll. A lot of teams started blitzing the pick-and-roll and jumping two guys at it to take the ball out of the hands of the point guard. He'd duck right between them and shoot that little runner in the lane. Nobody was doing that at that time. You watch an NBA game now, and almost everybody does that. Mark was a pioneer in that regard."

Cavs fans will never forget the game against the hated Detroit Pistons on February 28, 1989. Price was guarding Hall of Fame guard Isiah Thomas. As he ran around a pick by Pistons center Rick Mahorn, the latter almost decapitated Price with an elbow to the head. Price dropped to the court like a bag of hammers. He suffered a concussion and left the game with 6:10 remaining. No foul was called on the play, and Mahorn wasn't ejected.

The Cavs sent videotape of the play to the league office. The NBA fined Mahorn $5,000. "You can't tell me it was an accident," Cavs coach Lenny Wilkens said. "Mahorn could have seriously hurt Mark. This has to be addressed very strongly."

Price called the fine a "slap on the wrist." It was actually the largest fine to date for an elbow shot to the head. "Somehow this sort of thing has to be stopped, and I don't think a fine such as this is going to do it," he said.

Price missed the next game with the concussion. Some say Mahorn's cheap shot affected Price's career permanently. Cavs general manager Wayne Embry said it took Price a long time to recover from the elbow to his temple. The following season in Detroit, there was still bad blood between the two teams because of the incident. Embry jumped out of his seat and ran 10 rows down on the court to break up a skirmish between Cavs center Brad Daugherty and Pistons center Bill Laimbeer.

Secretly, Embry later admitted in the book *Inside Game: Race, Power, and Politics in the NBA*, he wished Mahorn or Laimbeer would have taken a swing at him. He wanted a piece of either of them, even though he was 55 years old at the time. Referee Billy Oates tossed Embry out of the game. He was fined $10,000 by the NBA for his actions.

LeBron James tied Price's all-time record of 4,206 assists heading into the Dallas game March 10, 2015. He said, out of respect to Price, he's going to quit passing the ball. "I'm not passing for the rest of the year," he joked. "I want to stay right there with Mark Price. I'm staying right there with the legend."

19 Cavs Trade Ron Harper for Danny Ferry

The Cavs trade of Ron Harper to the Los Angeles Clippers for forward Danny Ferry is arguably the most controversial deal in the history of the team. To many observers, Harper was the Cavs' answer to Michael Jordan, who was a major obstacle to the team in the playoffs. The Cavs sent Harper, first-round picks in 1990 and 1992, and a second-round selection in 1991 to the Clippers on November 16, 1989. Ferry and swingman Reggie Williams came to the Cavs.

The trade was a disaster from the start.

Harper, the Cavs' No. 8 overall pick in the 1986 draft, averaged 22.9 points during his rookie season. He also led the league in turnovers. Very few players in the league could do some of the things he could do on the court. He was an explosive player. However, the Cavs were concerned with the company he kept—namely some who had ties to drugs and gambling. None of this was ever proven, mind you. It was a lot of innuendo. "I never saw any of that stuff," Cavs coach Lenny Wilkens said. "I didn't buy into any of that."

Cavs general manager Wayne Embry and Wilkens were called to a meeting at the Sheraton Hotel at Cleveland Hopkins International Airport. They arrived to find Cavs owner Gordon Gund, team legal counsel Richard Watson, and Horace Balmer, head of NBA security. Balmer informed the group that Harper had been associating with known drug dealers, according to sources in the Drug Enforcement Administration. Soon afterward, Gund insisted that Embry trade Harper. He wanted him off his team.

After the deal was consummated, *Cleveland Plain Dealer* beat writer Burt Graeff showed up for practice. "Lenny was totally shocked," Graeff said. "He couldn't believe they made that trade."

Ferry was the No. 2 overall selection in the 1989 draft by the Clippers. The 6'10" Duke forward had won the Naismith Award for the 1988–1989 season, signifying the top player in college basketball. When the Cavs announced the trade, they referred to Larry Bird in the press release. Embry said he fought hard to keep that reference out of the press release, but to no avail. He didn't want Ferry to be portrayed as the "Great White Hope."

Ferry and agent David Falk warned the Clippers that he didn't want to play for them, but they drafted him anyway. He went to Italy to play for Il Messaggero (now Virtus Roma), which lured him away from the NBA with a $2 million-a-year salary. He was given the use of a five-story piazza, rent-free, along with a $75,000 BMW. After one season in Europe, he signed a staggering 10-year, $34 million deal with the Cavs. Despite that record-setting contract, Ferry proved to be a mediocre player at best. It didn't help that he came to one of the strongest teams in the league. Ferry had trouble getting regular minutes behind the front court of Brad Daugherty, Larry Nance, and John "Hot Rod" Williams. Some wondered if Wilkens ever had confidence in Ferry, who played sparingly.

Ferry also suffered from knee problems, which contributed to his woes. Ferry didn't reach double figures in scoring until his breakthrough season of 1995–1996 when he averaged 13.3 points. It was his sixth season in the NBA.

Wilkens is still bitter about that trade. "Ron was an integral part of that team," he said. "It cost us a chance to beat Chicago." Wilkens resigned from his position with the Cavs after the 1992–1993 season. Some suggested it was because of his torn Achilles' tendon suffered in the off-season. "I came back from that," Wilkens said. "I was upset we traded Ron Harper. The players liked Ron. When he'd walk into the locker room, it lit up. We had a chance [to win the championship]. The pieces fit. They all complemented each other."

Wilkens said Ferry was an outstanding collegiate player. However, in the NBA, he was nothing more than a role player. Wilkens had some regrets about leaving the Cavs. "I had all those guys as rookies," he said. "We enjoyed being around each other."

Wilkens truly believes the trade tore the heart out of the Cavs team. "Michael Jordan was a great player," Wilkens said. "But in my opinion, if we had kept Ron Harper, we would have gotten by them [in the playoffs]."

Harper, who later played for the Bulls, said he discussed the deal with Jordan. "Me and M.J. talked about this all the time," Harper told the *Chicago Tribune.* "He says, 'If they didn't trade you, who knows how good that [Cavs] team would have been?' I said, 'If they didn't trade me, I'd have one or two of your six rings.'"

When Harper showed up to the Richfield Coliseum as a rookie in 1986, reporters could barely understand him. He had a terrible speech impediment. He knew what he wanted to say. It just wouldn't come out. A native of Dayton, Ohio, Harper certainly wasn't the only NBA player who stuttered. Bulls forward Bob Love stuttered, as did former Cavs forward Barry Clemens. "[Love] couldn't get a word out of his mouth," Graeff said. "I felt so bad for this guy. It was awful. He got straightened out. The last I heard, he was working in the Bulls' front office."

Clemens, quite the outside shooter, poked fun at his impediment. Cavs coach Bill Fitch arranged some businessman luncheons at the hotel across the street from Cleveland Arena. "He'd always bring a player to the luncheon," Graeff said. "One day he brought Barry. He got up there and said, 'I'd like to tell you guys the highlights of my career. But I've only got an hour.'"

Clemens had a long professional basketball career. He said the expansion drafts prolonged his NBA career. He later became a successful stockbroker in Rocky River, a suburb of Cleveland. "That guy could shoot," Graeff said.

Harper went on to win five championship rings, three with the Chicago Bulls and two with the L.A. Lakers.

"I was never a great basketball player until I got over my speech problem," he said. "Getting my speech problem under control gave me confidence in myself, and then I had more confidence in my basketball game, too."

20 Cavs Become a Reality in 1970

Cleveland businessman Nick Mileti bought Cleveland Arena and the Cleveland Barons hockey team for $1.5 million in September 1968. He wanted to expand his sports empire and put in a bid for an NBA expansion team in 1970.

Cleveland was awarded an expansion team, along with Buffalo and Portland, in February 1970. The cost to join the NBA was $3.7 million—less than the average salary for a player in the league now. Mileti raised much of the money through a public sale of stock. The Cavs lost almost $800,000 in the first four years of the franchise—all

Cavs Begin Play at Cleveland Arena

The Cavs played their first four seasons at Cleveland Arena in downtown Cleveland. Their first season was 1970–1971.

The Arena was built and privately financed by local businessman Albert C. Sutphin during the Depression in 1937. Its first tenant was the American Hockey League's Cleveland Barons. The Cavs and World Hockey Association's Cleveland Crusaders, both owned by Nick Mileti, later played in the Arena, located at 3717 Euclid Avenue.

The Arena seated 9,900 fans. It was expanded to more than 12,000 for boxing events. The NBA's Cincinnati Royals also played some home games at the Arena before the Cavs became a reality.

The Cavs began their first season with 15 consecutive losses. They finished that season 15–67.

The Arena was outdated and broken-down by the time it closed in 1974. It was demolished in 1977. Opposing NBA players refused to shower at the Arena and oftentimes walked across the street to the team hotel in their warm-up jerseys after games.

"The visiting players hated it," Cavs radio announcer Joe Tait recalled. "They wouldn't even shower there. They stayed at the Sheraton across the street, changed in their rooms and walked into the arena wearing their uniforms.

"One winter, there was a tremendous snowstorm. It was almost a whiteout as I drove down Euclid to the game—and there was this purple thing in front of me. As I got closer, I realized it was Wilt Chamberlain in his Lakers uniform and warm-ups. Thank God I was going slow or I'd have killed him."

played at the decrepit Cleveland Arena. Mileti owned the Cavs for 11 years. He moved the team to the $36 million Richfield Coliseum in the fall of 1974. Frank Sinatra opened the spacious arena in October of that year.

Ted Bonda, an investor in many of Mileti's ventures, once called Mileti's athletic conglomeration "an empire built on marshmallows." "He built that Coliseum out of just plain air and he did a magnificent job," Bonda told the *Los Angeles Times*. "If he'd had a little more [cash], he might have been able to hold it together."

Cavs Owners
The following are Cavaliers owners through the years:

Nick Mileti, 1970–1980
Louis Mitchell, February 1980
Joseph Zingale, March 1980
Ted Stepien, April 1980–1983
Gordon Gund, 1983–2005
Dan Gilbert, 2005–present

Gib Shanley, a sportscaster at WEWS-TV 5 in Cleveland, said Mileti reminded him of a former sports owner in Cleveland. "Nick is not an administrator," he told the *L.A. Times*. "He's very good at putting the deals together and promoting the show....There's a little bit of Bill Veeck in him."

Veeck, a former owner of the Indians, once signed a midget and sent him to the plate for the St. Louis Browns. The Cavs, made up of misfits and castoffs from other teams, were horrible their first season in 1970–1971. They finished in last place with a 15–67 record.

"There was a reason they won 15 games," *Cleveland Plain Dealer* beat writer Burt Graeff said. "They played [fellow expansion teams] Portland and Buffalo 12 times each."

21 A Parade for the Ages

An estimated 200,000 people lined the streets in downtown Cleveland for the Indians' 1948 World Series celebration. They didn't even bother to have a parade for the Browns' 1964 NFL championship. Of course, they more than made up for that slight by having the biggest blowout of them all on June 22, 2016. As

LeBron James welcomes an estimated 1.3 million Cavaliers fans with open arms on June 22, 2016. He and his teammates were on their way to the rally to celebrate Cleveland's first major championship in 52 years.

many as 1.3 million fans came downtown for the Cavs' parade and rally to celebrate their first NBA championship.

The parade was choked to a crawl by the overflow crowd. Cleveland police were unable to keep fans on the sidewalks. They spilled out onto East Ninth Street, which didn't allow the convertibles carrying Cavs players to pass.

After hours went by, the players, coaches, and front office made it to Mall B where the stage had been set up. It ended with Browns Hall of Fame running back Jim Brown handing the Larry O'Brien Trophy to Cavs forward LeBron James, which signified that the city's 52-year championship drought was officially over.

"'It still hasn't hit me that this has happened," James said. "It's so surreal. For some crazy reason, I feel like I'm going to wake up and it's going to be Game 4 again."

The traffic was so badly snarled, the Associated Press reported that outgoing flights at Cleveland Hopkins International Airport were delayed because flight crews couldn't make it to their planes. It's a wonder that it was as orderly as it was with that many bodies in one area. A 13-year-old girl did get shot near Tower City late in the afternoon. The police department tweeted that the injuries to the female victim were not life-threatening, and that a teen was in custody afterward.

Wheelchair-bound Yianni Thallas had trouble seeing the parade in downtown Cleveland. Fans hoisted him and his wheelchair for a better view. "Awesome picture from the Cleveland parade yesterday!" Amherst city councilman Phil Van Theuren posted on his Facebook page. More than 1,000 people liked the post and another 1,000 shared it.

"We passed thousands of people who just wanted to help others and cheer on the Cavs," Thallas told the *Elyria Chronicle-Telegram*. "It wasn't just people helping the guy in the wheelchair. We set a great example for the rest of the world to show who Cleveland really is and how the fans are. It's pretty awesome." Thallas, 34, lives in Parma, but is an Amherst native. The picture was taken by Cleveland's Ryan Puente. Thallas was worried he wasn't going to be able to see the parade. "To be honest, I was concerned I wasn't going to see anything," he said. "I was concerned I was going to get trampled. I was worried, but it didn't really stop me."

At the beginning of the parade route at Quicken Loans Arena, James posed in front of his 10-story banner at the Sherwin-Williams building. The AP's Tom Withers wrote that James stood and posed with his arms outstretched just as he does on the giant mural—life imitating art—the photo op of a lifetime.

Coach Lue Gets the Call

When the phone rings and President Barack Obama is on the other end, you tend to listen.

A few days after winning the NBA championship, Cavaliers coach Tyronn Lue was in his office at Cleveland Clinic Courts in Independence when the president called to offer his congratulations. Obama invited Lue and the Cavs to visit the White House before the president leaves office.

The only stipulation? J.R. Smith probably has to wear a shirt.

Obama said he'd already reached out to LeBron James—of course—whom he said he knows. The president showed off his sense of humor in the four-minute call to Lue. "It didn't hurt having this guy named LeBron James," Obama said. He also said he was impressed with the play of point guard Kyrie Irving, whom he said came alive during the playoff run.

"I've got to give coaching some credit, man," the president said. "You should be proud of yourself. I really do think you brought cohesion, steadiness, and a focus to the team. It really showed itself. You should feel good about what you did."

Lue was humble and gracious, extending credit to general manager David Griffin and Cavs majority owner Dan Gilbert. "It was just unbelievable, and I thank those guys all the time for having the belief and confidence in me," Lue replied.

Obama said he no longer plays basketball, but encouraged the 39-year-old Lue to keep playing. The president had some fun with the latest fad among Cavs players. "Tell J.R. and everybody to put on a shirt," Obama said. "You can't just be walking around without a shirt for like a whole week. Now [Iman] Shumpert is taking off his shirt, Kyrie is taking off his shirt. C'mon, man."

James spoke for 17 minutes and thanked all of his teammates. He drew some criticism later when he dropped two F-bombs, which caught some area television stations off guard that had live broadcasts. Hopefully, the FCC will be lenient. It has been 52 years.

"I'm nothing without this city," he said. "I'm nothing without you all. Let's get ready for next year."

Hopefully, the celebratory parade is a thing every Cavs fan can do again in June 2017.

22 Cavs Acquire Nate "The Great"

Outsiders look at Nate Thurmond's statistics in his two seasons with the Cavaliers and wonder why his No. 42 is retired in the rafters of Quicken Loans Arena. He averaged 5.0 points and 6.3 rebounds in 114 games.

However, his numbers don't accurately describe his worth to the team. He came aboard on November 27, 1975, in a big trade with the Chicago Bulls. The Cavs sent center Steve Patterson and forward Eric Fernsten to Chicago in exchange for Thurmond and forward Rowland Garrett. The 6'11", 230-pound Thurmond was a force around the basket. He made his mark on the defensive end, blocking shots, altering shots, and pounding the boards. By the time he arrived in Cleveland, he was already 34 years old. He was only a shadow of his former dominant self—the player who battled Wilt Chamberlain, Bill Russell, and Kareem Abdul-Jabbar to a standstill for years.

He was beloved by the fans, largely because he was a local product. He played at Central High School in Akron and Bowling Green State University. Thurmond did most of his damage in 12 seasons with the San Francisco/Golden State Warriors. He was the third overall pick in the 1963 draft and played behind Chamberlain for a season and a half before Wilt was traded to Philadelphia.

Thurmond assembled some huge seasons with the Warriors, including 1967–1968 when he averaged 20.5 points and 22 rebounds. He was traded to the Bulls for center Clifford Ray prior to the 1974–75 season. Thurmond was never able to live up to the high expectations in the Windy City. Part of that thought process could have stemmed from his first game with the Bulls in 1974. He became the first player in NBA history to officially record a quadruple-double with 22 points, 14 rebounds, 13 assists, and 12 blocks against Atlanta. Blocked shots weren't counted before the 1973–1974 season.

He played just one full season in Chicago before being jettisoned to the Cavs just 13 games into the 1975–1976 season. It was a shrewd deal by Cavs coach Bill Fitch. The 1975–1976 roster was chock full of talented players and ready to take a major step as a championship contender. What it needed was veteran leadership. That's where Thurmond filled the void. He was the team's backup center behind Jim Chones. It was the perfect role for Thurmond, who was nearing the end of a stellar career.

"I remember it vividly because I wasn't fitting in well in the scheme of things in Chicago, and I didn't really like that set-up because it was really forward-oriented and I had to do some passing that I hadn't really done in my career," Thurmond told Cavs.com. "But to come home is always great. Especially, I think, it's a little easier at the end of your career. When you're younger, you might try too hard to impress people at home [and] you have too many distractions. But at that point in my career, I knew I was coming in to back up Jim Chones. And to be around my brother and my parents and some of the people I went to high school with was tremendous."

Thurmond knew he was coming to an accomplished team. "Well, they were young, but they were good," he said. "They had talent. You look at Bingo [Smith], you look at Austin [Carr], Campy [Russell], Jim Chones, Footsie Walker. And throw a couple veterans in there like Dick Snyder and Jim Brewer. They had a great team, no question about it. Defensively, I knew I could help with rebounding and knowledge of some of the people in the league. And Bill Fitch was great to me. He told me what he wanted from me. He told me, 'You're going to get 18 to 20 minutes a game.'"

The Cavs had instant karma. "The main thing, the guys that I just mentioned, they accepted me right away," he said. "I love those guys. I've never been on a team where I fit in more than with those guys. We came together and we had the best record after the All-Star break that year. We were rolling. We knew we were good, but we weren't overconfident."

Thurmond's high school career didn't end like many envisioned. Central High, which also featured future NBA star Gus Johnson, was undefeated before being upended in the Ohio high school tournament by Middletown. The Middies' Jerry Lucas was one of the most talented high school players in the history of Ohio, and that includes Akron St. Vincent–St. Mary's LeBron James. Lucas won two state championships with Middletown and compiled a 76–1 record. Lucas' presence affected Thurmond's college choice, as well. He didn't want to play behind Lucas, so Thurmond spurned a scholarship offer from Ohio State and enrolled at Bowling Green.

Thurmond brought notoriety to Bowling Green and improved the Mid-American Conference's stature. He was named first-team All-America by the *Sporting News* in 1963. After joining the NBA, he was unable to bring a championship to the Warriors or the Bulls. However, after being traded to Cleveland, his presence gave the Cavs legitimate championship aspirations. The Cavs were coming of age—in the standings and in the fans' hearts—after so many years of losing. Once they finally turned the corner, the fans' interest soared. They won their first Central Division title that year in what will forever be known as the "Miracle of Richfield."

They upended the Washington Bullets in the first round of the playoffs. They advanced to the Eastern Conference Finals against Boston but suffered a major setback in the week heading into that series. Chones broke a bone in his foot in practice and was lost for the rest of the season. That forced Thurmond into the starting lineup against the Celtics—a tall order for the aging center—with power forward Jim Brewer handling the backup center duties. The Cavs lost the series to Boston, four games to two. "We were one broken bone away from winning the NBA championship," Thurmond said.

He retired after the 1976–1977 season. He opened Big Nate's BBQ restaurant in San Francisco after briefly trying his hand at broadcasting. He died at age 74 on July 16, 2016, after a brief battle with leukemia.

Ricky Being Ricky

When the Cleveland Indians were in their heyday, there was a saying in Cleveland about their zany outfielder, Manny Ramirez. Whenever he would act out, people would say, it was just "Manny being Manny."

The same could be said about Cavs swingman Ricky Davis. One of the most talented and athletic players to appear in a Cavs' uniform, Davis had a way of getting under people's skin. That included several coaches he played for and against.

The Cavs hosted the Utah Jazz on March 16, 2003. The Cavs were putting the finishing touches on a 122–95 victory, and Davis was gunning for his first career triple-double. Utah's Scott Padgett scored with 7.6 seconds left. Davis took the inbounds pass and purposely missed a shot at the Jazz's basket in an attempt to secure his 10th rebound. Utah guard DeShawn Stevenson body-checked Davis after the boneheaded move.

Davis' antics drew the ire of Jazz coach Jerry Sloan, who wanted a piece of the Cavs player. "He was trying to embarrass us, and that's not how the game should be played," the old-school coach said. "This is not schoolyard basketball. Let him try to get it when the game means something."

Sloan, who handled many disagreements with his fists back in his playing days, said he was proud of Stevenson. "I would have knocked him down harder," the coach said. "They can put me in jail for saying that, but that's the way it is."

Stevenson said he couldn't let Davis disrespect the game. "I have nothing against Ricky," he said. "But for someone to go out there and do that is not right. I'm not going to let that happen."

Davis was stopped outside the Cavs' locker room after the game. He said one of his teammates yelled out that he needed one more rebound for a triple-double. "[The Jazz] should be mad," Davis said. "Any team that gets beat that badly shouldn't be happy. But I wouldn't do it again. I just wouldn't. I'd probably be mad, too, losing by 20."

It turned into a national controversy. Several national columnists condemned Davis' antics. He earned the nickname, "Wrong Way" Davis. "I did some bad things, but the only thing I regret is my triple-double," he told NBA.com. "But everything else comes with experience."

Now years later, everyone knows it was just "Ricky being Ricky."

24 Cavs Acquire Brad Daugherty in 1986 Draft

Some would say it was the worst trade in the history of the Philadelphia 76ers. Sixers general manager Pat Williams was on his way out of town. His last act was to deal the No. 1 pick in the 1986 draft to the Cavs for forward/center Roy Hinson and $800,000.

The Sixers were three years removed from an NBA championship. They needed an infusion of young talent to complement Julius Erving. Instead of keeping the top pick and building around North Carolina center Brad Daugherty, they shipped the rights to the No.

1 selection to the Cavs on the eve of the draft on June 16, 1986. The 76ers thought Daugherty was soft.

Not keeping the talented 7′, 263-pounder became a bigger farce when the Sixers decided to deal center Moses Malone to the Washington Bullets for Jeff Ruland in a separate deal. Ruland played five games for the Sixers in 1986–1987 before a foot injury derailed his career. He retired for the next four seasons before attempting an ill-fated comeback.

Hinson, a 6′9″, 220-pounder, lasted a little longer in Philadelphia. He played a season and a half before being traded to New Jersey. He would never live up to his potential in the NBA.

Daugherty, now a broadcaster for ESPN, became arguably the best center in Cavs history. The five-time All-Star averaged 19 points, 9.5 rebounds, and 3.7 assists in eight seasons in Cleveland. The Cavs were without a general manager heading into the draft. Barry Hecker, the Cavs' director of player acquisition, and Ed Gregory, a West Coast scout, were credited with making the deal with Sixers owner Harold Katz. Williams, Philadelphia's GM, bolted for the Orlando Magic the next day.

The 76ers had salary-cap problems, but there was another issue. "Who would you rather have: Brad Daugherty or Roy Hinson?" Katz told the Associated Press.

Years later, of course, it turned into a major blunder. "We really liked Roy," Hecker told the *Cleveland Plain Dealer*. "But he was really the only player of value we had that we could trade."

Cavs president Thaxter Trafton said the team needed to get bigger. "The feeling on our staff is that the Eastern Conference is much bigger than in the past, and you have to get big people to compete with Boston, New York, and Atlanta," he said. "We felt [Daugherty] was the best player available and the best big man available."

When back problems forced his retirement after the 1993–1994 season, Daugherty was the Cavs' all-time leading scorer (10,389 points) and rebounder (5,227). The Black Mountain, North

Carolina, native was just 28 years old when he played his last NBA game.

The Cavs' public relations department got Daugherty on the phone on draft night to speak to the Cleveland media. When he thanked Wayne Embry for drafting him, things got a bit awkward. The conference call was quickly aborted.

Embry will go to his dying day insisting he didn't do anything underhanded, even though he was a consultant and employed by the Indiana Pacers on the night of the draft. He had accepted the Cavs' general manager position but wanted to stay through the NBA Draft on June 17, 1986.

Cavs owner Gordon Gund called Embry on the eve of the draft and said the team might be leaning toward drafting Maryland forward Len Bias with the No. 1 pick. Embry informed Gund that Daugherty was the best pick for the Cavs. Of course, he had no idea Bias would die days later of a cocaine overdose.

Getting Daugherty was just the first step in the right direction. Former GM Harry Weltman's controversial second-round pick from 1985, Tulane center John "Hot Rod" Williams, was cleared to play in the NBA. He sat out the entire 1985 season for his involvement in the Tulane point-shaving scandal. The Cavs made the announcement on draft night that he was eligible to play.

The Cavs drafted Miami of Ohio shooting guard Ron Harper with their own first-round pick, eighth overall, and selected Richmond swingman Johnny Newman with their second-round pick. They also traded a 1989 second-round pick and cash to the Dallas Mavericks for Georgia Tech point guard Mark Price. He was selected by the Mavericks with the 25th overall pick.

"After the draft, I knew, based on everything I'd heard, that this would be one of the great drafts of all time," Gund told the *Cleveland Plain Dealer*. "To be able to fill practically your whole starting team was special. It was great for the city. It was a phenomenal turnaround."

Cavs' 1986 NBA Draft

Round	Overall	Player	College
1	1	Brad Daugherty	North Carolina
1	8	Ron Harper	Miami (Ohio)
2	29	Johnny Newman	Richmond
3	50	Kevin Henderson	Cal State–Fullerton
4	73	Warren Martin	North Carolina
5	96	Ben Davis	Gardner-Webb
6	119	Gilbert Wilburn	New Mexico State
7	142	Ralph Dalton	Georgetown

Hecker said the Cavs wanted to shake things up. "We're sending the message to the league that we're not dead, that we want to win," he said.

Largely because of the 1986 draft, the Cavs embarked on their most successful run at that point in the franchise's history. "It was significant," Embry said later. "That set the stage for the team in the late 1980s and early 1990s. In our opinion, we thought we were the best one-through-12 team in the league. We just couldn't overcome that one obstacle—Michael Jordan."

Trafton, who ran the Coliseum, said the Cavs were being aggressive. "Anyone can stand pat," Trafton said. "But our basketball people analyzed it and decided they wanted to do what they did. They didn't want to hold back."

The Cavs struck it rich—and did so without the benefit of having a GM on board. Weltman was fired after three years on the job. Many think he doesn't get enough credit for pulling the franchise out of the Ted Stepien doldrums. "Ted brought in Harry to start the cable TV thing," *Akron Beacon Journal* beat writer Larry Pantages said. "SportsChannel had started in New York, and Ted said that's what the Cavs needed to do. Harry had some cable experience in New York City, as well as being the GM of the [ABA] St. Louis

Spirits. Harry talked Ted into hiring him to run the TV side of it, but gradually became his confidant on the basketball side."

There are many close runners-up for the best drafts in Cavs' history, including 2003 (LeBron James), 1971 (Austin Carr), and 2011 (Kyrie Irving). However, none could come close to the 1986 draft.

25 Dan Gilbert Buys Cavs for $375 Million

Gordon and George Gund earned a good return on their $20 million investment in 1983. They announced the sale of the Cavaliers and Gund Arena to Michigan billionaire Dan Gilbert on March 1, 2005, for a reported $375 million.

Gilbert is founder and chairman of Quicken Loans, the nation's largest online mortgage company. He was introduced at a press conference at Gund Arena, flanked by R&B artist Usher, a minority investor; David B. Katzman, Gilbert's first cousin and vice chairman of Quicken Loans; and Gordon Gund.

Gilbert immediately broke the ice. "Has the check cleared yet?" Gilbert jokingly asked Gund. "We're going to have exciting times here," the 42-year-old Gilbert said. Gordon Gund retained a reported 15 percent ownership stake in the team. Gilbert's brother, Gary, is another minority owner.

Game highlights were shown on video screens behind the dais. Usher's Grammy-winning song, "Yeah!" was cranked up. Gilbert's most famous and highest-paid employee, LeBron James, sat in the crowd. "I wish I could have a beer with LeBron to celebrate, but I can't," Gilbert said of the 20-year-old James.

"We like to execute," Gilbert said. "We're not bureaucracy-type people. We don't need committees and long-winded negotiations to come to conclusions. We want to make this the best franchise in professional sports. We're in the bowels of business; we'll build it, and the money will follow."

Gilbert's company is based in Livonia, Michigan. He has no plans to move to Ohio. He said he can fly to Cleveland on his private jet in 22 minutes. After buying the team, rumors surfaced that Gilbert tried to pass coaching suggestions to coach Paul Silas during a game. He was politely told that isn't proper protocol. Gilbert wanted to replace Silas as coach soon after the former took over ownership of the team. Silas was eventually fired with 18 games left in the 2004–2005 season and replaced by interim coach Brendan Malone.

Gilbert and Katzman revamped the entire organization. Employees that survived say it's not out of the ordinary to receive emails from Gilbert and Katzman at all hours of the night. They take particular interest in Fox Sports Ohio's broadcasts of the Cavs' games. Gilbert quickly replaced longtime play-by-play broadcaster Michael Reghi with former Pistons announcer Fred McLeod, who was paired with analyst Austin Carr.

Gilbert was extremely lucky in the NBA's draft lottery, winning three times in a span of four years with Kyrie Irving, Anthony Bennett, and Andrew Wiggins. In 2013 Gilbert decided to bring an all-star cast to New York for good luck at the lottery. The group included former Browns quarterback Bernie Kosar, Browns cornerback Joe Haden, R&B artist and Cleveland native Machine Gun Kelly, and WKNR-850 AM radio host Tony Rizzo.

After the Cavs prevailed in the lottery, giving them the No. 1 pick in the draft, Rizzo was fired up. "Yeah!" he exclaimed from the stands.

Rizzo spotted NBA commissioner David Stern and wanted to share his enthusiasm. "David, we did it!" he said. Witnesses were shocked by the outburst. The stoic Stern was not amused.

26 Visit the Naismith Memorial Hall of Fame

Wayne Embry was born in Springfield, Ohio, in 1937. He was inducted into the Naismith Memorial Basketball Hall of Fame in Springfield, Massachusetts, as a contributor to the sport. Embry long served as a trustee for the Hall of Fame.

"I always wondered what it would feel like to be here," he said during his induction speech. "Well, I'm here. Needless to say, I am overwhelmed by my own emotions as I speak. I can't think of any individual honor that is better."

Embry played 11 seasons in the NBA, winning a championship in Boston in 1968. He was a two-time Executive of the Year in 1992 and 1998 with the Cavs. He was the first black general manager in NBA history in Milwaukee, and the first black president in the league in Cleveland. "I spent my life trying to do the right thing for the game," he said. "I was involved in different facets of the game, different committees, and USA Basketball. I was a Hall of Fame trustee for a number of years. Anything for the growth and development of the game, you just do it. You don't do it to be recognized. I felt good about it."

Embry joined the Cincinnati Royals in 1958. "I've been involved in some capacity ever since," he said. He's currently a consultant with the Toronto Raptors, marking his 58th year in the NBA. "There's not much I haven't seen," he said. "I try to stay out of the way. I'm not the GM. I'm available."

He said his family always encouraged him to be successful and not to be afraid to fail. "They allowed me to remain humble and not let anyone take my dignity," Embry said. "Whenever possible, I give back to the game of basketball and try to make an impact."

The Hall of Fame opened in 1959 when it honored its first class. There are 361 coaches, players, referees, and contributors who are enshrined, as well as 10 teams. All of the enshrinees are honored for their outstanding achievements and accomplishments. As the highest honor in basketball, entrance into the Hall of Fame recognizes outstanding contributions to the sport.

The Naismith Memorial Basketball Hall of Fame is located in the "Birthplace of Basketball," Springfield, Massachusetts. According to the Hall of Fame's website, the city is easily accessible from no matter what direction from which you are traveling. The museum is conveniently located within driving distance from New York, Boston, and Hartford, Connecticut, and is right off of Massachusetts Route 91. For those who are travelling by air, the museum is easily accessible from Logan International Airport in Boston and Bradley International Airport in Hartford.

Accommodations are centrally located throughout Springfield, with several hotels within five minutes of the Hall of Fame, located at 1000 Hall of Fame Avenue. Hotels available in Springfield include Marriott, Hilton Garden Inn, Sheraton, LaQuinta Inns and Suites, Hampton Inn, and Residence Inn, among others.

The Hall of Fame was originally housed on the campus of Springfield College, where the game was first played on December 21, 1891. That day, a physical education instructor named James Naismith introduced a new game to his class of 18 young men at the YMCA International Training School in Springfield.

The Hall offers the 60 Days of Summer program. Family-oriented programming is offered for almost two months—from June 29 to August 30. The Hall will host various appearances, autograph signings, magicians, trick dribblers, jugglers, mascot days, and giveaway days.

Tickets are $23 for adults, $17 for seniors, and $16 for children five to 15 years old.

27 LeBron Wins First MVP in 2009

Not only did LeBron James win the league's most prestigious individual award, he did it at home. James was presented the Maurice Podoloff Trophy, indicative of the league's MVP. He chose to accept the award at St. Vincent–St. Mary High School in Akron on May 4, 2009.

"To be voted most valuable player of the NBA is unbelievable," James said. "This is a place where all my dreams started and where I thought they could become real. There's really not a better place."

He received 109 of a possible 121 first-place votes to easily outdistance Los Angeles Lakers guard Kobe Bryant. James totaled 1,172 points in balloting by media members in the U.S. and Canada. "People asked me the last two days, how do I feel?" he said. "I don't know because it's an individual award and, if you know me, individual accolades, I never really get high on them. This is like a team award. Individual accolades come when team success happens."

James became the first Cavs player to win the MVP award. He helped the Cavs to an NBA-best 66–16 record. He averaged 28.4 points, 7.6 rebounds, and 7.2 assists a game that season. The entire Cavs team sat in the crowd, in addition to family members, former teachers, former coaches, longtime friends, and hundreds of St. Vincent–St. Mary students.

He arrived at his old school in a Ferrari with a police escort. "I'm 24 years old and I'm receiving this award," James said. "I never thought it would happen this fast. I never dreamed about being MVP, but if I said I didn't enjoy this award I'd be lying to you. Hard work pays off and dreams do come true."

LeBron James and his mother, Gloria, show off his trophy after LeBron was named the NBA's Most Valuable Player in a ceremony at LeBron's alma mater, Akron St. Vincent–St. Mary High School, in Akron, Ohio, on May 4, 2009.

He was presented a Kia SUV for winning the award. He donated it to the Akron Urban League. "He's never forgotten where he came from," mother Gloria James said. "I'm very proud of him. It is long overdue, and he's real deserving of it."

James also earned the MVP award in 2010, becoming just the 10th player in NBA history to win back-to-back MVP awards. He also brought home MVP awards with the Miami Heat in 2012 and 2013.

During his first season back in Cleveland in 2014–2015, he finished third in the voting behind Golden State's Stephen Curry and runner-up James Harden of Houston. Cavs coach David Blatt couldn't understand why James' name wasn't more prominent in the MVP race. "That's just kind of funny, to be honest with you," Blatt said. "First of all, he's the greatest player in our game. You don't have to look very far at our record to see what impact he has on this team when he's playing and not playing. Certainly it does say something about what his value is when he is absent, what happens to the team. Obviously, if we look at our own example, then you're looking at an MVP player in every respect, which is not news to anyone."

There were more than a few whispers around the league that James had lost a step earlier in the season. That's one reason he decided to rest for those eight games. "I don't really get involved in what people say about the way I approach the game," James said. "It made no sense for me to talk about it until I crossed that path. It got to a point where I knew that I just had to give my body a rest. My body told me it needed a rest, and it's paid off for our team."

If James were to win another MVP trophy, he'd be joining some select company. Michael Jordan and Bill Russell are the only two players in history to have won five MVP awards. Kareem Abdul-Jabbar sits all alone atop league history with six MVPs.

"I have to be the MVP for these guys, the guys in this locker room," James said after the Cavaliers dismantled the Golden State Warriors February 26, 2015, 110–99. "When I'm on the floor, I try to do everything I can to help us win—offensively, defensively, whatever the case may be. Wherever I end up [in MVP voting] at the end of the season, that's where it's at."

Cavs forward Kevin Love really put his foot in his mouth when he was asked on the *Dan Patrick Show* whom he'd vote for MVP on

March 23. Strangely enough, he didn't pick James. "They're both having an MVP-type season," he said, "but I'm going with Russell Westbrook."

When he has an MVP candidate on his team, in the same starting frontcourt, you would think his answer would have been a little different. There are ways to answer that question. The way he answered it opened up a Pandora's Box.

Love's answer fosters questions about his relationship with James. "You know, we're not best friends," Love said on ESPN radio's *Mike & Mike* show.

Again, that wasn't how to answer that question, even if it's true. Kobe Bryant and Shaquille O'Neal spent several years ruffling feathers with the Los Angeles Lakers, yet won three NBA championships. They don't have to be bosom buddies.

James said after practice on March 24 at Cleveland Clinic Courts, he didn't think too much about Love's comments. "I don't really get involved in that," he said. "The voters are going to decide who is MVP. What Russ has been doing, his numbers have been pretty crazy keeping those guys afloat in the West with his play. "Steph Curry can make a case for sure with what he's been doing, James Harden, and myself as well. Kev has his own opinion who he believes is MVP. No one should fault him for that."

James said voters shouldn't compare this season to his previous MVP seasons. "When I'm on the floor, you judge me by when I'm on the floor and by winning," he said. "Do I win? When I'm on the floor, am I playing at a high level? That's all I care about. When I'm on the floor, is my team winning? That has a lot to do with it and how my numbers when I'm on the floor. Judge me by that and then when I'm not on the floor."

Love said he wasn't surprised by all the attention his appearance on the *Dan Patrick Show* generated. "[Not] if you choose to get the little three- or four-second clip of my whole answer," he said. "I said LeBron could very well be the MVP, [along with] Steph Curry,

James Harden. Those are guys you all talk about and you know very well all of them could be the MVP."

Love said it had been a media circus all season. "Yes, just because we know all of you also know this is probably one of—if not the biggest—stories in sports with LeBron James coming home," he said.

28 Willoughby Leads Cavs Past Lakers in 4 OTs

The scene was a cold, snowy night in Ohio on January 29, 1980. The Cavs were bumbling through yet another losing season—their first without coach Bill Fitch. They hosted the eventual NBA champion Los Angeles Lakers in front of 13,820 at the Coliseum.

It turned out to be perhaps the greatest regular season game in Cavs' history. Forward Mike Mitchell put the finishing touches on a 34-point night with two free throws with two seconds left in the fourth overtime in the Cavs' 154–153 victory.

The Cavs, coached by Stan Albeck, set a franchise record for points. The combined points by the two teams were also a team record. Former Cavs center Jim Chones, who had been traded to the Lakers on October 5 for center Dave Robisch and a third-round pick, fouled out on the last play.

The Cavs had trouble dealing with Lakers center Kareem Abdul-Jabbar that night. The 7′2″ future Hall of Famer finished with 42 points, 17 rebounds, and nine blocks. By the end of the game, he was being guarded by journeyman Bill Willoughby. Willoughby, a 6′8″, 205-pound forward, kicked around the league for eight seasons. He played 78 games for the Cavs in 1979–1980. The Cavs ran out of big men to guard Abdul-Jabbar. Willoughby, one of the first players to enter the league directly from high school, eventually drew the impossible assignment. Willoughby was from the era of the prep-to-pros phenomenon that also included Moses Malone and Darryl Dawkins. Willoughby refused to let the Cavs' reserves lose that game.

Mitchell finally helped the Cavs prevail in the fourth overtime. "[I] just had to stop the game," he told the *Cleveland Plain Dealer*. "I knew I had to make both free throws."

Robisch, formerly Abdul-Jabbar's understudy, realized the significance of the marathon game. "I don't know if this was the best game I've ever been in, but as far as excitement and thrills go, it definitely was the best game," he said.

29 "Am I Speaking Chinese?"

The Cavs were playing in a hotly contested game at The Palace of Auburn Hills (Michigan) on December 16, 2004. Cavs guard Eric Snow committed an eight-second backcourt violation and coach Paul Silas immediately yanked him out of the game. Silas sent Jeff McInnis into the game to replace Snow.

As the fiery Snow walked past Silas on his way to his seat, he muttered something under his breath. It's unclear if he cursed at his coach or he was just upset by the situation. Nonetheless, Silas blew up. Silas demanded that Snow get off the bench and sent him to the locker room. He didn't play in the second half of the Cavs' 81–69 loss.

It was a heated topic in the postgame press conference. Silas answered questions about the incident, three or four different ways. One could tell he was losing patience. A reporter from the *Columbus Dispatch* asked one more Snow question and Silas blew a gasket. "Am I speaking Chinese?" he bellowed. The young reporter hadn't

One of the Great Outbursts of All-Time

Cavaliers coach Paul Silas had a temper. He came from an era when players often settled disagreements with their fists.

The Cavs faced the Atlanta Hawks at Philips Arena on November 22, 2003. Cavs forward Ira Newble had played the previous two seasons with the Hawks before signing with the Cavs as a free agent. Cavs general manager Jim Paxson offered both Newble and swingman Eric Piatkowski half of the mid-level exception that summer. Whichever free agent accepted it first would play for the Cavs.

The November 22 game in Atlanta was a big deal to Newble, who had several family members in attendance. He also lived there in the off-season. After the Hawks' 92–83 victory, reporters were mulling around the locker room. I was interviewing Zydrunas Ilgauskas when the door to the coach's office slammed behind me. Everyone turned in that direction and saw Newble storm out of the coach's office, with Silas a few steps behind.

I headed out of the locker room. Silas was screaming at Newble, who was hightailing it down the hall. Newble was upset with his lack of playing time and had let the coach know about his displeasure. Silas called Newble, among other things, a "hip-hop mother——." If Newble hadn't vacated the area, there would have been fisticuffs.

The look in Silas' eyes was pure rage. He was ready to throw down, despite being 60 years old at the time. He was one of the toughest players in the league back in the day. He admitted about a week later he probably would have been no match for Newble if things had escalated into a fight.

"He would have kicked my ass," Silas joked.

done anything wrong. He was just in the wrong place at the wrong time. Driving home from Detroit the next morning, the talk radio shows had a field day with the quote, playing it over and over again.

Silas suspended Snow for one game and docked him one game's pay—about $54,000. It ended his streak of 248 consecutive games played. "We're moving on," Snow told the Associated Press. "Things happen, unfortunately. I apologize to coach. I apologize to the fans and the team, so there is no need to dwell on it. It's an unfortunate incident. It was a misunderstanding, but he's still the coach and he's still allowed to make the decisions that he wants to make, and players got to live with it. He's the coach. Everybody gets upset when they come out of the game, but there's no need to show frustration."

Snow struggled with the thought of telling his son, E.J., why his father wasn't playing in the next game. Without Snow, the Cavs lost to Boston 114–107 in overtime. "I told him, 'Daddy had a disagreement with the coach and that he respects the coach and listens to the coach,'" Snow said. "He said, 'Oh, okay, Daddy.'"

Snow was one of five players nominated in 2003 for the NBA's J. Walter Kennedy Citizenship Award, given for outstanding community service.

Cavs Hire Wayne Embry as GM

Wayne Embry was named the first African American general manager in professional sports in 1972 when he was hired by the Milwaukee Bucks. After hiring a close friend, Don Nelson, as Milwaukee's coach, Embry felt that his coach had stabbed him in the back. Nelson won a power struggle with Embry, who found himself out of a job.

He wasn't out of work long. He became a part-time consultant with the Indiana Pacers. However, while scouting for the Pacers on the eve of the 1986 NBA Draft, Embry was approached by the Cavs about their vacant GM position. They had fired Harry Weltman, who many thought did a good job in Cleveland, bringing stability to the woebegone franchise and helping it emerge from the Ted Stepien abyss.

Embry accepted the job before the draft, yet stayed with Indiana through the draft. He helped with the Pacers' selection of Chuck Person with the No. 4 overall pick. Pacers owner Herb Simon informed Embry that he was hiring Donnie Walsh as the team's president and

GM. While still under the employ of the Pacers, Embry was giving advice on who the Cavs should select in the draft. The Cavs traded for the No. 1 pick in the draft and selected North Carolina center Brad Daugherty. While talking to the Cleveland media on a teleconference on draft day, Daugherty thanked Embry, which raised some eyebrows. Of course, by then, it was the worst secret in town.

The morning of the draft, Cavs owner Gordon Gund called Embry to inform him the trade for the top pick had been finalized. They sent forward/center Roy Hinson and cash to the 76ers. "We have some mixed reviews on who we should take," Embry said he was told by Gund. "Some think we should take Len Bias."

Embry said he would have had no idea Bias would be dead of a drug overdose within days, but his gut feeling was that something was amiss with the Maryland star. "Gordon, please take Daugherty," Embry told the Cavs owner. "I have some reservations about Bias. I think there are some character issues."

The Cavs finally signed off on Daugherty.

They also selected Miami of Ohio shooting guard Ron Harper with the eighth overall pick. They traded for Georgia Tech point guard Mark Price in the second round—a player the Pacers were also interested in acquiring.

Embry worked on a trade with the Mavericks for that second-round pick—in his role as Pacers' executive—but the Cavs beat Indiana to the punch and drafted Price. Simon pulled Embry outside the draft room and gave him a tongue lashing. Embry said he hadn't been admonished like that since growing up on his grandfather's farm in rural Ohio.

More awkwardness.

Simon later tried to get a draft pick from the Cavs as retribution for them missing out on Price. The Cavs resisted and insisted they had done nothing wrong. Embry was introduced as the Cavs' GM the day after the draft. He would be the Cavs' GM for 13 seasons. Jim Paxson replaced him in 1999.

31 Cavs Fire David Blatt Mid-Season

It was an extremely bold move, firing a coach whose team had the best record in the Eastern Conference.

That's exactly what Cavaliers general manager David Griffin did on January 22, 2016, when he dispatched coach David Blatt. He guided the Cavs to a 30–11 record, yet was fired.

Blatt has far and away the best winning percentage (.675) of any Cavs coach in franchise history—in fact, if you exclude Tyronn Lue's .659 mark over half a season, the next closest mark is coach Mike Brown at .620. Blatt was 83–40 in his season-and-a-half as coach. He guided the Cavs to the 2015 NBA Finals, where they lost four games to two to the Golden State Warriors. After that season, there were some whispers that he could be in trouble, but they were quickly dismissed. Perhaps there was some validity to the rumors after all.

Blatt was the first NBA coach to be fired with his team atop its conference since the league began conference play in 1970, the Elias Sports Bureau reported. When Blatt was fired, the Cavs were 3½ games ahead of Toronto for the top spot in the East. Blatt became just the third coach since 1977 to be fired in the season following their teams' appearances in the NBA Finals. The other coaches were New Jersey Nets coach Byron Scott in 2004 and Philadelphia 76ers coach Gene Shue in 1977.

The Cavs were dismantled by the Warriors 132–98 on January 18, 2016. That couldn't have helped Blatt's cause. He was replaced as coach by his top assistant, Tyronn Lue, the highest-paid assistant coach in NBA history at a reported $1.4 million per year. Lue, a finalist for the job when Blatt was originally hired in June 2014, signed a reported five-year, $35 million contract on July 26, 2016.

Blatt, a highly successful coach in Europe before he came to Cleveland, was named the Eastern Conference Coach of the Month for October and November combined in 2015.

Cavs general manager David Griffin made the controversial move to fire Blatt. He cited a "lack of fit with our personnel and our vision" and explained: "What I see is that we need to build a collective spirit, a strength of spirit, a collective will. Elite teams always have that, and you see it everywhere. To be truly elite, we have to buy into a set of values and principles that we believe in. That becomes our identity."

Griffin admitted that the move could blow up in his face. Of course, it didn't, as Lue guided the Cavs to their first ever NBA championship.

Griffin said he believed the Cavs didn't have the right mentality. "I have never seen a locker room not be as connected after wins as they need to be," he said. "We've only been galvanized when expectations were not high."

Griffin said he's more confident Lue has the pulse of the team. "This is not an indictment of David Blatt as a coach," Griffin said. "And it's not to say that Ty Lue is a better basketball coach. He's a better basketball coach for this team today."

After the move was made, Griffin called Lue. Cleveland.com reported that Lue's response might not be what Griffin had expected.

"This is f—— up, Griff," Lue reportedly said.

Griffin pleaded with Lue. "What's done is done," he reportedly said. "I'm asking you if you can lead this team?" Lue said he could lead the team. Griffin then congratulated his new coach.

The GM insists that LeBron James had nothing to do with the controversial move. James said he was informed of the decision when he showed up to the team's practice facility on January 22. "I didn't talk to any of the players before this decision," Griffin said.

David Blatt argues a call during his last game as head coach of the Cavaliers, a 115–102 win over the Los Angeles Clippers on January 21, 2016, in Cleveland. Blatt's .675 career winning percentage is best among all Cavs head coaches.

"It's really critical to me for everybody to understand this is my decision. This is our basketball staff's decision....I'm not taking a poll." Griffin said it was an insult to him to infer that James had that much power on the team.

Cavs owner Dan Gilbert supported Griffin's move. "Over the course of my business career I have learned that sometimes the hardest thing to do is also the right thing to do," he said.

Dallas Mavericks coach Rick Carlisle, president of the NBA Coaches Association, said Blatt's firing made him "embarrassed for our league."

Blatt took the high road in a tweet sent out by his agent. "I am very grateful to have had the opportunity to serve as the head coach of the Cleveland Cavaliers," Blatt said in the statement. "I'd like to thank [owner] Dan Gilbert and David Griffin for giving me this opportunity and am honored to have worked with an amazing group of players from LeBron James, Kyrie Irving, and Kevin Love through our entire roster. I'd also like to express my extreme gratitude to my coaching staff. I am indebted to them for their professionalism, hard work, loyalty, and friendship. I am proud of what we have accomplished since I have been the head coach and wish the Cavaliers nothing but the best this season and beyond."

32 LeBron's 48-Point Outburst in Playoffs

LeBron got hot—scorching hot—and the Detroit Pistons could do nothing to stop him. James' 48-point outburst in Game 5 of the Eastern Conference Finals on May 31, 2007, was unparalleled in Cavs' playoff history. What made the 109–107 double-overtime victory more special was that it occurred at The Palace in Auburn Hills, Michigan.

James had 48 points, but only two three-pointers in the game. He played 50 of the 58 minutes in the game. He made 18-of-33 field goals, 2-of-3 from behind the three-point arc and 10-of-14 from the foul line. He added nine rebounds, seven assists, and two steals. He scored 29 of the Cavs' last 30 points in the game, including their last 25. More importantly, the victory gave the Cavs a 3–2 edge in the best-of-seven series.

James was exhausted by the time he came to the postseason press conference. "I'm banged up," he said. "I'm winded. I'm fatigued. I've got all day tomorrow. It's going to be tough to get some rest when you got a crazy two-year-old running around the house. So, hopefully, I can take him to one of his grandmas' houses."

James, who scored the game-winning layup with 2.2 seconds left, got in a zone and continued to attack the Pistons. He was the only Cavs player to convert a field goal in the last 17 minutes, 48 seconds.

The Pistons tried to trap him and get the ball out of his hands. The strategy didn't work. "We threw everything we had at him," Pistons guard Chauncey Billups said. "We just couldn't stop him. It's frustrating. He put on an unbelievable display out there. It's probably the best I have seen against us ever in the playoffs."

James carried the team on his shoulders. "I was able to will my team to victory," he said.

Cavs coach Mike Brown was in awe of James' performance. "Somebody told me in the locker room that he scored 29 of our last 30 points, and I could not believe it," he said. "Everybody keeps asking for more, and he keeps giving more. I feel bad that my words don't do justice for what he did."

33 Lenny Wilkens: The Ultimate Hall of Famer

Lenny Wilkens was named to the Naismith Memorial Hall of Fame three times: as a player in 1989, as a coach in 1998, and for his part in coaching the U.S. Olympic team in 2010. The former

Cavs point guard Lenny Wilkens (19) scores his 17,000ᵗʰ pro point in a game against the Bullets on February 12, 1974. The Hall of Famer was an All-Star for the Cavs and later became the team's head coach.

Providence star was also inducted into the College Basketball Hall of Fame in 2006.

He was hired as the 10ᵗʰ coach in Cavs' history on July 9, 1986. Unfortunately, he never took the Cavs to the NBA Finals, despite having superior talent. Wilkens did guide the Seattle SuperSonics to their only championship in 1979 as coach.

The left-handed point guard played two seasons for the Cavs. He made the All-Star team—the last of nine selections in his stellar career—during the 1972–1973 season. After the 1973–1974 season, the Cavs sold Wilkens' contract to Portland. He finished his 15-year NBA career as a player-coach with the Trail Blazers in 1974–1975.

Wilkens was one of 40 player-coaches in NBA history. He also was a player-coach for three seasons in Seattle from 1969 to 1972. When he played for the Cavs, the media portrayed him as being a coach out on the court. Maybe it was because he actually had been. "I couldn't do justice to both [jobs]," Wilkens said. "I wanted to spend more time teaching. I had an advantage being a guard and knowing the game more than everyone else. I was always running the show [as a point guard] even in practice."

The NBA's last player-coach was Boston's Dave Cowens in 1978–1979, and there hasn't been one since. The league prohibited player-coaches when it instituted the salary cap for the 1984–1985 season. It didn't want teams to circumvent the rules since coaching salaries don't count on their salary cap.

Wilkens was brought in to coach the Cavs by general manager Wayne Embry. It was incorrectly thought that they were joined at the hip. That wasn't the case. "I don't think they had any serious problems," *Cleveland Plain Dealer* beat writer Burt Graeff said. "Lenny was not real tight with a lot of people. He kept his distance. He was very introverted. He could be a little standoffish."

Wilkens assigned one of his assistant coaches, Dick Helm, with the task of reading the papers and reporting back to him. Helm was credited with helping Cavs forward Larry Nance develop a deadly perimeter jump shot toward the end of his career. "Dick would read all the stories and report back to Wilkens," Graeff said. "Half the stuff [he told him] was wrong."

Wilkens played pickup games with the writers and PR staff, which showed the major difference between rec league players and NBA talent. "He would show you little things like throwing a pass right over the top of your head," Graeff said. "He was a tremendous player for a number of years."

The coaching staff would play against the reporters on media day. That kind of frivolity is long gone.

34 "I'm a Heat Now"

Valuable Cavs forward/center John "Hot Rod" Williams became a restricted free agent in the summer of 1990. The Cavs had several intense contract negotiating sessions with Mark Bartelstein, Williams' Chicago-based agent. However, Williams shocked the Cavs by signing a six-year, $24 million offer sheet with the Miami Heat. That was an astronomical amount for that era.

Heat part-owner and president Billy Cunningham called Cavs general manager Wayne Embry to inform him they signed Williams to the offer sheet. He told Embry he hoped the offer sheet was more than the Cavs could afford, according to Embry.

Cunningham knew the Cavs' salary structure and gambled that they wouldn't pay Williams more than their starters. The 6'11", 245-pound Williams was convinced he was heading to South Florida. "I'm a Heat now," he said. "They did not want me. I'm a Heat."

The Cavs had 15 days to match the offer. This was a team capable of competing for an NBA championship. They couldn't let one of their key pieces walk. The problem with matching the offer was that Williams—the Cavs' sixth man—would make more money than Brad Daugherty, Larry Nance, and Mark Price, the team's established stars.

Before the Cavs matched the offer, they made modifications to the contracts of Daugherty, Nance, and Price, just to keep harmony in the locker room. The Cavs ended up matching the offer, which threw their salary cap out of whack for years to come. Williams became one of the highest-paid players in the NBA and wasn't even a starter.

Williams died of prostate cancer at age 53 on December 11, 2015.

He's No Robin

When the Cavaliers signed guard Larry Hughes to a lucrative deal on August 2, 2005, they finally thought they had found a running mate for LeBron James. The Cavs tried unsuccessfully to find the No. 2 punch to James, then an emerging star. Cavs general manager Danny Ferry signed Hughes, an unrestricted free agent, to a five-year, $70 million contract—one of the largest in franchise history.

There were other viable options, including Suns guard Joe Johnson. Because he was a restricted free agent, he was pretty much bypassed by the Cavs. If they had signed him to an offer sheet, the Suns would have the option of matching the offer. They also had interest in Bucks guard Michael Redd and SuperSonics guard Ray Allen. Hughes pulled up the rear in comparison to the other three candidates.

Johnson was a seven-time All-Star in Atlanta and Brooklyn. Redd, an Ohio State product from Columbus, was a 19.0-point career scorer. He made the All-Star team in 2003–2004. Allen, a future Hall of Famer, won NBA championships in Boston and Miami. He's made more three-pointers than any player in history.

And then there was Hughes.

He averaged 14 points in his 13 NBA seasons. Hughes just couldn't live up to the hype with the Cavaliers. He had trouble staying healthy, and he also had to deal with the heart-related death of his younger brother during the Cavs' playoff run in 2006.

Hughes missed 58 games in his two full seasons with the Cavs. He was part of a three-team, blockbuster trade on February 21, 2008, as 11 players changed hands. The Cavaliers acquired Ben Wallace, Joe Smith, Wally Szczerbiak, and Delonte West in the megadeal.

Ferry certainly tried to turn the Cavs into a contender in the summer of 2005. He signed free agents Donyell Marshall, Damon Jones, Zydrunas Ilgauskas, and Hughes. They got one trip to the NBA Finals in 2007 out of the free-agent bonanza.

36 Delonte West Goes Commando

Things changed forever for Cavs guard Delonte West when he was arrested after driving a three-wheeled motorcycle on the Beltway with three loaded guns in his possession on September 19, 2009. He was driving a Can-Am Spyder when he cut off a Prince George canine officer near Route 214 in Maryland. West was pulled over for making an unsafe lane change, but the tenor of the stop changed when West told the officer he had a gun in his possession.

The officer actually found three guns—a Beretta 9mm in West's waistband, a Ruger .357 Magnum strapped to his leg and a shotgun in a guitar case slung over his back, according to a spokesman for Prince George's police department. He also had a bowie knife.

Police charged West with two criminal counts of carrying a handgun for the Ruger and the Beretta, and issued him a traffic citation for driving "in excess of reasonable and prudent speed," court records show. West was within his rights to carry the shotgun and knife.

West's father, Dmitri West, inferred that his son was being chased. "All I can say is Delonte was looking behind his back and protecting himself," he told the *Washington Post*.

West spoke at media day at Cleveland Clinic Courts in Independence on September 28, 2009. He tried to downplay the incident and said he has been told by his lawyer not to talk about what happened. Things completely broke down thereafter, as he didn't speak to the media the rest of the season. News leaked that he had a mood disorder. Several news outlets reported he was bipolar and suffered from depression.

The season before the incident, he'd also quit talking to the media. While at a practice gym in Chicago, I tried to talk to him about it after getting clearance from PR person Amanda Mercado. He was sitting on the other side of the gym, all by himself, staring off into space when I approached him. "It just doesn't matter what I have to say," he told me.

After the gun incident, it became an us-vs.-them situation. When Associated Press reporter Tom Withers walked by West in the locker room and said hello, West erupted in anger. None of us reported the incident.

West was missing days of practice, presumably to attend counseling sessions. He lost his starting job at shooting guard to free-agent acquisition Anthony Parker. It was crystal clear this would be his last season in Cleveland. There were too many distractions regarding West. He had married his college sweetheart two months before the gun arrest. A month later, they got divorced. That could have contributed to many of his problems.

Perhaps the most damaging and insensitive rumor was that West was having an affair with LeBron James' mother, Gloria. There is no evidence that it was true. In a fantastic story by David Haglund on *Slate*, West said when people are chuckling about James' mom and the gun-laden motorcycle ride, you're laughing at a human being— "a person who plays basketball," not just a basketball player. But the LeBron rumor, coupled with claims that West was unstable, pretty much ended his NBA career. He tried using the National Basketball Development League as an avenue back into the NBA. It didn't work. West's odd sense of humor turned off some people.

Cavs general manager Danny Ferry originally tried to get his hands on West during the 2005 NBA Draft. He was unsuccessful in trading for West's rights. He was drafted by Boston with the 24th overall pick in the first round. Ferry eventually landed the 6'3", 190-pounder at the trade deadline on February 21, 2008, when the Cavs completely reshaped their team in a three-team deal. They brought in West, Ben Wallace, Joe Smith, and Wally Szczerbiak.

He became a starter on a Cavs team that eventually lost to Boston in the Eastern Conference semifinals in seven games. West played more minutes in that series than any Cavs player other than James. West also had the second-most assists and was third in scoring.

West was a free agent that summer, and negotiations were difficult between the Cavs and his agent. There was a rumor that West would play for Dynamo Moscow in Russia. I immediately shot down the rumor after talking to an agent that had talked to Moscow coach David Blatt, who would later become the Cavs coach in 2014.

West finally signed with the Cavs for about $4 million per season, with a team option for a third year. That's about the time he told reporters that he needed help. "In a sense, you feel like a weaker man, because you have to raise your hand and ask for help," he was quoted as saying. "But I found out over the last week that it made me a stronger person. I came back focused, and with the help of some medicine and talking with people on a regular basis, I'm back in good spirits."

He was honest and open about his problems. It turned out to be a mistake, since very few NBA players admit to any kind of weakness. On the night of his arrest, Haglund reported that West said his mother informed him he had to do something with the weapons he had in his house after his cousins had gotten into a closet where they were stored. That led to him transporting the weapons to another location.

West pleaded guilty to two misdemeanors, unlawfully carrying a dangerous concealed weapon and unlawfully carrying a handgun, and he was sentenced to house arrest, unsupervised probation, counseling, and community service.

After losing to Boston in the playoffs—and losing James in free agency—the Cavs declined West's option on his contract. He ended up signing a one-year unguaranteed $1.1 million deal with the Celtics. West was suspended by the NBA for the first 10 games of the 2010–2011 season. He missed much of the season with a broken wrist. He ended up playing just 24 games with the Celtics that season. He played 44 games for the Dallas Mavericks in 2011–2012, which signaled the end of his NBA career.

37 Larry Nance: The Human Pogo Stick

Larry Nance is probably best known for beating out Julius Erving as the first winner of the NBA's Slam Dunk Contest in 1984. It wasn't until the Phoenix Suns traded him to the Cavs in 1988 that his high-flying career really took off. He joined a power trio in Cleveland that included center Brad Daugherty and guard Mark Price, and helped the Cavs reach new heights.

Nance's shining moment came on January 7, 1989, against the New York Knicks when he blocked 11 shots. The Cavs had 21 rejections overall in their 101–96 win at Richfield Coliseum.

Upon his retirement in 1994, the 6'10", 235-pounder was the top shot-blocker in NBA history for a non-center. The three-time All-Star averaged 17.1 points, 8.0 rebounds, and an astounding 2.2 blocks per game in his 13-year career. He's the only player in Cavs' history to make the All-Defensive team three times. That includes his first-team selection in 1988–1989. His No. 22 jersey was retired by the Cavs.

The 11 blocks are a Cavs' franchise record, and six off the NBA's all-time mark. Former Cavs center Elmore Smith once blocked 17 shots while playing for the Los Angeles Lakers against Portland on

Cavs forward Larry Nance (22) slams over the Nets' Chris Dudley in Cleveland's series-clinching 98–89 first-round playoff victory in New Jersey on May 1, 1992.

October 28, 1973. He blocked an NBA record 11 shots in a half, including six in one quarter.

The Nance story came full circle on June 25, 2015. His son, Wyoming forward Larry Nance Jr., was a first-round pick of the Los Angeles Lakers.

"There wasn't a whole lot of [attention] going on with him," Lakers coach Byron Scott told the *Akron Beacon Journal.* "Then, after every workout he had, he just started being one of those guys that people started thinking about."

The Lakers were impressed in three areas—his athleticism, energy, and basketball IQ. It sure didn't hurt that he was the son of the former NBA standout. "I love him [as a player]," Scott said. "He's pretty good with the ball as far as decision-making."

38 Long-Distance Champs

Thirteen times in the history of the event, the Cavs had participants in the Three-Point Contest during All-Star weekend. On three occasions, they came home champions. Mark Price won back-to-back titles in 1993 and 1994, and Kyrie Irving brought home the first-place trophy in 2013.

Irving wanted to dispel all the doubters at the Toyota Center in Houston that year. "I just want to go out and prove a point that I was one of the premier shooters out there with all these guys," he said. Irving held off challenger Matt Bonner of San Antonio in the finals, 23–20. His winning round was two points off the record of 25 shared by Craig Hodges in 1986 and Jason Kapono in 2008. Price had 24 in 1994.

It was almost a coming-out party for Irving in 2013. "I feel like I'm a better off-the-dribble shooter than a spot-up shooter," he said.

"I'm not sure how many threes I have on the year, but not as many as the guys I was shooting against out there. I try to be as efficient as possible."

Irving also scored 32 points in the Rising Stars Challenge in 2013, as well as 15 points in his All-Star debut. "This weekend was just basically about earning everybody's respect and people getting a chance to see me that don't usually see me," Irving said. "We're not nationally televised. This weekend is to show my face to the fans and get everybody acclimated to my face in the league."

Irving finished fourth in 2014. Celtics great Larry Bird won each of the first three Three-Point Contests from 1986 to 1988. Price, the pride of Enid, Oklahoma, was a 40 percent three-point shooter in his 12-year career. He slipped past Portland guard Terry Porter in the 1993 Three-Point Contest finals in Salt Lake City, 18–17. Price connected on 16 of 25 shots, including his first seven attempts. Then he had to sweat out Porter's performance in the final round. Luckily for Price, Porter missed every shot in his last rack of balls.

"He was shooting well and I was happy when the clock ran out," Price said of his close call. Price was eliminated in the first round in each of his previous two years in the competition. He tried to stay relaxed in 1993. "I've never won before, so I didn't have great expectations coming in," he said. "I hit a couple shots early, and that really helped out."

Craig Hodges' dream of a fourth consecutive title evaporated in the semifinals when Porter slipped past the former Chicago Bulls guard 17–16. Porter, a late replacement for the injured Dennis Scott of Orlando, made the most of his opportunity. He made 11 of his first 15 shots in the finals against Price, but faded down the stretch. "I wasn't shooting well and didn't even get the money ball off on time," Porter said.

I didn't attend the festivities in Salt Lake City. I was working in the office at the *News-Herald*. After Price won the crown, Cavs PR director Bob Price (no relation) walked over to him, handed him a phone, and I interviewed him about his accomplishment. It was a different world. There weren't 2,000 media members from all over the globe covering All-Star weekend.

The following year in Minneapolis, Price blew away challenger Dana Barros of the Philadelphia 76ers in the finals 24–13. "I feel like I'm one of the best shooters," Price said. "But there are a lot of great shooters that don't necessarily shoot threes. Every arena I went to [last year], it was like all I could do was shoot threes. I can do a lot more than that."

Barros won the coin flip and had the option to shoot first in the finals. He decided to let Price shoot first, which proved to be a grave mistake. Price made 15 of his first 16 shots, which psyched out his challenger.

Price wasn't sure what he was going to do with the first-place prize of $25,000. "You'll have to ask my wife [about] that," he said.

39 "Win a Ring for the King"

Shaquille O'Neal might not have had much left in the tank when he arrived in Cleveland, but no one could dispute the fact he was a global icon. The 7'1", 325-pounder has the gift of gab. He was a fun guy to be around.

The Cavs finally pulled the trigger on the long-talked-about trade with the Phoenix Suns on June 26, 2009. They sent swingman Sasha Pavlovic, center Ben Wallace, and a 2010 second-round pick to the Suns. They started intense discussions at the trade deadline in February, but rumors said they didn't want to part with promising youngster J.J. Hickson at the time. After falling short in the 2009 Eastern Conference Finals to the Orlando Magic, Cavs general manager Danny Ferry rekindled talks with his good friend, Suns GM Steve Kerr. They were both former teammates with the Cavs. In hindsight, had the Cavs had O'Neal in the Magic series, perhaps Dwight Howard wouldn't have torn through their front line like tissue paper.

Ferry even asked me my thoughts on acquiring O'Neal. I replied that O'Neal wasn't the Shaq of old, but he was still better than half the big men in the league, even at 37. From a marketing standpoint, interest in the Cavs would be sky high if they made the deal.

They made the big trade the day after the NBA Draft. O'Neal didn't make it to town for his introductory press conference at Cleveland Clinic Courts until July 2. He did things at his own pace. He said his motto was, "Win a ring for the King," referring to LeBron James, his new teammate. "That's what I'm here to do," O'Neal said. "This kid right here is special. He's been very humble. He's made a name for himself. He'd done it the right, respectful way. For me, I'm honored to play with the great LeBron James."

The 2009–2010 Cavs had some firepower with James, guard Mo Williams, forward Antawn Jamison, and center Zydrunas Ilgauskas. "We definitely have all the pieces here," O'Neal said. "There will be no excuses. Expectations are very high. We want them to be high. That's what motivates us."

Ilgauskas would now be coming off the bench, and he was fine with the move. "I've always been high on Shaq, and he's the best center I ever played against," Ilgauskas said. "So if anyone is going to replace me in the starting lineup, then I don't mind it being him at all. Somebody else is going to have to guard him in practice, or I won't last until Christmas."

O'Neal, one of the all-time greats in the NBA, defended his game. "I think I have a lot left," he said. "There are only four or five real good centers in the league. I'm in that [group]. I'm very intelligent. I'm playing with a player that can make the game very easy for me."

O'Neal had several nicknames over the years—Shaq, the Big Aristotle, Diesel, and Shaq Daddy, to name a few. Perhaps there would be a new one—the Big Freeze—now that he was in Cleveland.

The 15-time All-Star, four-time NBA champion, and former MVP wasn't able to get it done in his lone year in Cleveland. He earned $20 million in 2009–2010, and the Cavs made little attempt to bring him back in the summer of 2010. He averaged 12 points and 6.7 rebounds in 53 games. The Cavs suffered a bitter upset to the Boston Celtics in the Eastern semifinals, four games to two. Things became even more desperate that off-season. Along with O'Neal, GM Danny Ferry, coach Mike Brown, and King James all left the team after the loss to the Celtics.

One day after practice during the regular season at Cleveland Clinic Courts, O'Neal held court with the media. As we dispersed, the gentle giant stopped behind *Akron Beacon Journal* beat writer George Thomas. He wrapped his giant arms around him from behind, and shook his belly. We all got a good laugh out of it.

Another time in Indianapolis, Cavs physical therapist George Sibel was in the locker room to stretch O'Neal before the game. Once again, O'Neal was in a playful mood. Sibel tried to stretch Shaq's tree trunk of a leg, but the center put a nifty reverse move on him, and the two were wrestling in the middle of the locker room. Sibel might weight 180 pounds at the most. He was holding his own with the 325-pound Shaq, before the behemoth finally got the best of him.

40 LeBron's Clutch Shot Stuns Bulls

Then Cavs coach David Blatt had a rough stretch in Game 4 of the Eastern Conference semifinals against the Chicago Bulls on May 10,

2015. After Bulls guard Derrick Rose tied the score at 84 with a driving layup with 9.4 seconds left, Blatt stepped onto the court and tried to call timeout. Assistant coach Tyronn Lue pounced on Blatt and pulled him toward the bench. The Cavs were out of timeouts, and had the officials noticed Blatt's gaffe, he would have been assessed a technical foul. It could have cost the Cavs the game.

"Yeah, I almost blew it," Blatt said.

Cavs forward LeBron James had his layup attempt blocked by Bulls forward Nikola Mirotic with 1.5 seconds left. Blatt then drew up the final play on his grease board. There was only one problem. It didn't fly with James. "Give me the ball and get out of the way," he was quoted as saying in the huddle.

Guard Matthew Dellavedova passed James the ball in the corner, and he drained a 21-foot, game-winning jumper over Bulls guard Jimmy Butler at the buzzer. Teammates mobbed James at midcourt after he had stunned the Bulls 86–84 to even the hard-fought series at 2–2.

Blatt inexplicably drew up the final play for James to take the ball out of bounds and pass it to one of his teammates. James overruled his coach. James likened it to a great quarterback like Peyton Manning or Tom Brady checking off at the line of scrimmage. It wasn't insubordination. It was James' gut feeling. "I'm not inbounding the ball," he said. "We're going to win or lose with me. I'm going to take that responsibility. In my eyes, it was [the right thing to do]. My team respects me to make decisions. It's no different than a great quarterback calling an audible."

James said he hadn't made many changes that season. "It's not about me changing play calls or Coach Blatt trying to call timeouts," James said. "We're a team. Players make the majority of the mistakes and coaches make mistakes. That's why we have our assistant coaches to help Coach Blatt when things aren't going right."

Blatt wouldn't say who was supposed to take the last shot in his version of the play. He said it wasn't J.R. Smith. "We thought

From the corner with time about to expire, LeBron James drills a game-winning, 21-foot jumper over the Bulls' Jimmy Butler in Game 4 of the 2015 Eastern Conference Semifinals in Chicago, evening the series at two games apiece.

about a couple different things, then honestly it came down to what LeBron thought was the best option based on his feeling on how he was being guarded, and we went with that," he said. "He made a great shot."

Blatt said he encouraged that kind of input. "Of course," he said. "The guys are in the fray. They are in the battle. He had a real strong feeling about catching the ball in a catch-and-shoot situation. It was the right play to make."

He said because of James' size and the fact that he's their best passer, he was going to opt for the four-time MVP to inbound the ball. Earlier in the season, in the San Antonio game, Blatt had James inbound the ball to Kyrie Irving. Perhaps, he was going to do it again. Irving, though, was dealing with issues with both legs. He had inflammation in his left knee and a strained right foot.

Blatt refused to say James vetoed the play. "He just felt strongly about what a better situation would be," he said. "It turned out it was the right play."

James said his relationship with Blatt was continuing to grow. "I've known my wife since 11th grade," James said. "It never stops growing when you're around someone every day. He's our general. I try to be an extension of him on the floor."

Blatt said it was par for the course for him to take heat for the last play and for almost calling a timeout he didn't have. "A near-mistake was made," he said. "I owned up to it. An NBA coach makes 150 to 200 critical decisions in each game. That is paralleled only by a fighter pilot. If you do it for 20 some years, you're going to blow one or two. I blew one. Fortunately, it didn't cost us. As far as the play that was called, that wasn't fair."

He said it's part of the drama of a playoff series. "That's just part of our wonderful business we're all in," Blatt said. "It's 2–2 in the series. It's a heck of a series. We're all glad to be a part of it. There's nothing wrong with being critiqued. That means people think something of you and your program. Since Day 1, we've been very much under the microscope. My players and staff have never given in to the adversity that we've faced this year—major injuries, great expectations from a brand-new team. Here we are fighting like hell to make the Eastern Conference Finals. That speaks volume of the guys we have here."

The Cavs ended up winning the last three games of the series to win it, four games to two, and advance to the conference finals.

41 Ted Stepien: Incompetency at Its Finest

Ted Stepien almost single-handedly ran the Cavs out of town. He owned the team for three years and might have been the worst owner in the history of professional sports. His reign of error began in 1980 and ended when the Gund Brothers stepped in and purchased the club in 1983. In the process, they fleeced Stepien by acquiring the Cavs, Richfield Coliseum, and Nationwide Advertising for $20 million.

In the end, Stepien went out exactly the way he came in: a total mess.

Stepien's first move turned into a monumental disaster. He shipped guard Butch Lee and the Cavs' first-round pick in 1982 to the Los Angeles Lakers for forward Donnie Ford and the Lakers' 1980 first-round pick. Two years later, the Lakers selected North Carolina power forward James Worthy with the first overall pick in the 1982 draft. Worthy, of course, became a Hall of Famer and one of the top power forwards in the history of the game.

Things only got worse. Stepien, along with his first lieutenant, Bill Musselman, had a weird infatuation with trading first-round picks to the Dallas Mavericks in exchange for mediocre talent. It got so bad, the league had to step in to put a stop to it. The Cavs sent four unprotected first-round picks to Dallas from 1983 to 1986 in three separate deals. They received Mike Bratz, Geoff Huston, Richard Washington, and Jerome Whitehead in those deals. Meanwhile, the trades helped the Mavericks become a solid playoff team.

The deal with the Lakers was franchise-altering. The trade with Dallas on October 30, 1980, was almost as damaging. According to folklore, the Cavs had agreed to trade the disgruntled Bill Robinzine to the Mavericks for Washington. Then Cavs coach Musselman decided he had to get his hands on the 6'10", 220-pound Whitehead, who had averaged 5.3 points in the first seven games that year in Dallas. It was one of those cases where it would have been great to be a fly on the wall. Musselman offered two first-round picks for the former Marquette center. At that point, the front-office executive with the Mavericks supposedly put his hand over the phone, and repeated the offer to the other officials in the room. They all burst out in laughter. He took his hand off the receiver and informed the Cavs that Dallas would be able to "sacrifice" Whitehead for two first-round picks.

Mavericks coach Dick Motta later got in on the fun. "I was afraid to go to lunch for fear that I'd miss a call from Cleveland," he said sarcastically.

The Cavs got a lot out of that major trade. Whitehead, the player Musselman just had to have, managed one field goal in his three games with the Cavs. He was waived on November 17—just 17 days after the trade. The headline in the *Akron Beacon Journal* caused a stir: "Whitehead Deal Totals: No. 1 + No. 1 = 0."

Oh, by the way, those two first-round picks the Cavs sent to Dallas turned out to be guard Derek Harper in 1983 and forward/center Roy Tarpley in 1986. It was right about that time that NBA commissioner Larry O'Brien made an unprecedented move on November 6 when he announced the league was putting a halt to all of Stepien's moves. Before the Cavs could make a trade, they had to get it approved by the NBA's director of operations Joe Axelson.

O'Brien later ruled that no team could trade first-round picks in consecutive years. It became known as the Stepien Rule.

"I deeply resent the commissioner's conduct," Stepien told the *Cleveland Press*. "It is unprecedented. It is unfair. Nobody is more dedicated than me to bringing Cleveland a winner."

The Cavs landed the 1981 All-Star Game at the Richfield Coliseum. O'Brien showed up for a luncheon before the game, and Stepien had a long line of dignitaries on hand to greet him. Included in that group were the Cavs' cheerleaders, the Teddi Bears.

Among the cheerleaders was Stepien's daughter, Nancy, whom he introduced to O'Brien.

"Nice tits, huh?" Stepien supposedly said.

O'Brien was floored.

The league ended up taking over the complete operation of the All-Star Game that year.

Terrible Ted also hired Don "the Boot" Buttrey, who crushed beer cans with his teeth and blew up firecrackers in his mouth. Stepien changed the team's fight song to a polka and delivered copies of it to Cleveland area radio stations with a pound of kielbasa. His worst move—and perhaps the most unforgivable sin as far as the fans were concerned—was to allow radio broadcaster Joe Tait to leave town.

Stepien was unhappy with the criticism he was receiving from both Tait and, more specifically, talk-show host Pete Franklin. Franklin, host of the popular *Sportsline* on the 50,000-watt WWWE-AM 1100, believed Stepien was running the Cavs into the ground. He conducted on ongoing feud with Stepien, who was incensed by the criticism. After Stepien unsuccessfully tried to sue Franklin and the station, a decision was reached to end the agreement between WWWE and the Cavs.

Tait was caught in the crosshairs. Since he was technically employed by WWWE, he found himself out of work. He left to find other employment in the NBA. Fans protested and staged a rally in Tait's honor. When Gordon Gund bought the Cavs, one of his first moves was to bring back the games to WWWE and rehire Tait for the 1983–1984 season. Bringing back Tait was one of the smartest PR moves he ever made. The fans loved Tait and considered him a part of the Cavs' family.

"He is the franchise," Gund said. "To have a basketball team in Cleveland, you have to have Joe Tait."

Kobe Wearing Wine & Gold?

Heading into the 1996 NBA Draft, the Cavs had two first-round picks—No. 12 and No. 20—and needed size in the worst way. They eventually chose Wright State forward/center Vitaly Potapenko with the 12th selection and Lithuanian center Zydrunas Ilgauskas with the 20th.

The 12th pick came from Washington in a trade for guard Mark Price. Cavs center Brad Daugherty had retired at age 30 due to back problems two years before. The Cavs concentrated their attention on big men in the draft.

They worked out four centers in preparation for the draft: Potapenko, Ilgauskas, North Carolina State center Todd Fuller, and Mississippi State center Erick Dampier. Yet they were tempted by a prep prospect from Lower Merion High School in Ardmore, Pennsylvania.

Guard Kobe Bryant, son of former NBA player Joe "Jellybean" Bryant, was entering the league from high school. Cavs general manager Wayne Embry had a clear disdain for the preps-to-pros phenomena. But he couldn't shake the idea of drafting Bryant.

Bryant's agent, Arn Tellem, was reportedly working behind the scenes trying to dictate where his client would end up. Tellem was reportedly informing several teams Bryant wouldn't play for them, and the Cavs might have been one of them. Bryant spent much time in Europe while growing up when his father played for several Italian teams. Playing overseas might not have been a legitimate option for Bryant, but his agent might have planted that idea in the heads of several NBA general managers. That might have scared off some teams in the draft.

Tellem reportedly laid the groundwork for a trade that would ensure that Bryant would play for the "Showtime" Lakers. The Lakers sent center Vlade Divac to the Charlotte Hornets for the No. 13 pick, which they used on Bryant. The trade to the Lakers wasn't officially announced until July 11, 1996.

The Cavs had the option of trading the No. 12 pick for Divac, but nixed the move. They also could have made the risky move of drafting Bryant—and lived with the circumstances. Bryant, of course, became a five-time NBA champion with the Lakers and one of the league's all-time greats.

43 "Sheed Must Bleed"

There weren't many players more hated in Cleveland than Detroit Pistons forward/center Rasheed Wallace.

During the Cavs-Pistons' rivalry, sometimes things got a bit heated. It came to a head on February 26, 2006, during a game at The Palace of Auburn Hills, Michigan. While driving to the basket, Wallace elbowed Cavs center Zydrunas Ilgauskas in the head just 1 minute, 47 seconds into the game. It caused a bloody gash on the top of his head. Five stitches were needed to close the wound. Wallace, a villain in the eyes of Cavs fans, was slapped with a flagrant-1 foul and later fined $5,000 by the NBA.

Wallace later admitted that he elbowed Ilgauskas on purpose. "Why would I crack that cat in the skull to start the game if I wasn't elbowed first?" Wallace asked.

Ilgauskas returned to the game—a 90–78 loss—but was largely ineffective. He said he might have caught Wallace with an elbow to start the game. "I think [Wallace] was frustrated because I caught him first with an elbow and then he hit me back," Ilgauskas said. "Mine wasn't intentional. His…I didn't see the replay."

Cavs coach Mike Brown lobbied that Wallace should have been given a flagrant-2 foul. That would have meant an automatic ejection and a possible suspension. "I thought it was the wrong call," Brown said. "I thought Rasheed got upset and hit him on purpose. It didn't look from my vantage point that he went for the ball."

That's where the "Sheed Must Bleed" campaign started. Talk radio was ablaze the next day and a half. Fans wanted retaliation, and they didn't have to wait long to get it. The two Central Division rivals played the following night at Quicken Loans Arena. The following night went much like the day before, as the Pistons won 84–72. None of Ilgauskas' teammates retaliated for the cheap shot. In the old days, Wallace would have been pummeled. But Ilgauskas did stand up for himself, much to the delight of the crowd. He hip-checked Wallace and knocked him to the court. Wallace received a technical foul for laughing at Ilgauskas' "retaliation."

Of course, Wallace found a way to get under the fans' skin once more. "[There's] no laughing in basketball," he said sarcastically. "It's a serious sport or you're going to get thrown out."

The boorish Wallace was also known for his "guaransheed" predictions. He predicted the Pistons would beat the Cavs in the 2006 playoffs. Even though his timeline was a bit off, he ended up being right.

Wallace retired in 2013 and remains the NBA's all-time leader in technical fouls and ejections. He received a record-setting 41 technicals during the 2000–2001 season.

44 World B. Free's Grand Entrance

When World B. Free signed as a free agent with the Cavs in September 1983, he arrived to the outdoor press conference at the Richfield Coliseum in a helicopter. PR director Harvey Greene was credited with the clever stunt.

However, Greene said it was Cavs general manager Harry Weltman's idea. Owner Gordon Gund lent his support—and money. Greene took the idea and ran with it. "We had two goals—to get him here as quickly as possible and to get him signed," Greene said. "We brought him in on a red carpet. People still remember that. He landed in the parking lot of the Richfield Coliseum."

Free took his physical, signed his contract, and joined his teammates on the practice court later that day. "There was a time element and a PR element," Greene said. "It was a tight time frame. I said it would be a great media event. It would show the urgency of getting him here and see how much we wanted him back."

When he came off the helicopter, he was wearing the Cavs' new uniform. "All of a sudden, out of the sky came this chopper," *Akron Beacon Journal* beat writer Larry Pantages said. "And, boom, it sat down, and he jumped out. He said, 'I'm never doing that again.'"

Pantages said Cavs director of player personnel George Karl was sent to Brooklyn to locate Free. "When he came back, he said, 'I was in parts of New York that I didn't know existed. I was worried I wasn't going to get out alive,'" Pantages said. "George had to be the ambassador to get the deal done."

Some say Free saved the franchise. Greene doesn't agree. "The Gunds saved the franchise," he said. "World had a lot to do with that. The team was struggling at the time. He was the one bright spot. He was our one marquee player on a nondescript team. He was one of the most popular athletes in the city. To let him go would have been the wrong thing to do. Signing Free was a priority for the franchise." Greene said the free-agent signing invigorated the franchise.

The Cavs had just emerged out of the Ted Stepien era—and the team was on shaky ground. It was hemorrhaging money. The team hosted a draft party in June in a downtown Cleveland hotel. "We brought in a satellite truck to show the ESPN telecast," Greene said. "We were trying to do things the right way—for the first time. For us, it was critical to do things right. Ownership wanted to do things professionally and open their pocketbook. It was a new day in town."

The Cavs wanted to distance themselves from Stepien's bumbling ways. "What happened was, I was becoming a free agent, and the Gund brothers had just got the team and said that they were going to do something special," Free told Cavs.com. "I was back in Brooklyn. I remember them calling my agent and my agent telling me they're going to send a private jet. So I thought, *Private jet? I've never been in a private jet before.* But if they wanted to send a private jet, that was fine. So I got on the jet that flew into Cleveland. So now I'm thinking somebody will just pick me up and drive me down to the Coliseum. But they bring me from the private jet out to this here helicopter. I'm walking outside, looking at this helicopter—and it looked like one of those cartoon helicopters, like you'd wind a rubber band to make it fly. The propeller is going around and it's a two-seater—me and the pilot. The first thing I did was kiss my girlfriend. Because I didn't think it was going to make it."

Free was uneasy flying in the helicopter. He got real nervous after talking to the pilot. "I asked him, 'How long have you been flying?' He said, 'I just got my license yesterday!' He was laughing and he said, 'Just kidding.'"

Looking back on the day, Free realized it was something special. "I don't think anyone else has done that in NBA history," he said. "I asked all around the league—Dr. J, Michael Jordan—they all knew about it."

Free came to the Cavs from the Golden State Warriors on December 15, 1982, in exchange for shooting guard Ron Brewer. "World came in the middle of [Cavs coach] Tom Nissalke's first year," Pantages said. "Harry Weltman was able to dump Ron Brewer on Golden State—a straight one-for-one. He talked [Warriors coach] Al Attles into giving up on World."

Brewer was a wildly inconsistent player. "[Akron native and Bullets forward] Gus Johnson called Brewer 'Boot Head,'" Pantages said. "He said his head was shaped like a boot. Brewer would go for 30 points one night, eight the next night. If you didn't run a play for him early and get him going, he'd just disappear. There was no consistency. He was one of three great players who played at Arkansas for [coach] Eddie Sutton." Brewer, Marvin Delph, and Sidney Moncrief were known as "the Triplets." They helped the Razorbacks go undefeated in the Southwest Conference in 1977–1978 and made it to the Final Four.

Free averaged 23 points per game in his four seasons with the Cavs. "I've always been one of those guys who says World B. Free's number should be retired," said Joe Tait, voice of the Cavs.

"Bingo!"

Bobby "Bingo" Smith was one of the Cavs' most electric long-range shooters. Unfortunately, he played during the era before the three-point shot was instituted. The three-point shot didn't come to the

Cavs Retired Jerseys

Player	No.	Date Retired
Nate Thurmond	42	December 18, 1977
Bingo Smith	7	December 4, 1979
Austin Carr	34	January 3, 1981
Larry Nance	22	January 30, 1995
Brad Daugherty	43	March 1, 1997
Mark Price	25	November 13, 1999
Zydrunas Ilgauskas	11	March 8, 2014

NBA until his last season, 1979–1980, when he split the season between the Cavs and San Diego Clippers.

Fans remember two things about the former Tulsa standout. The first thing was his signature Afro. The other thing that separated him from his teammates was his ability to shoot the ball. His rainbow jumper from the corner was legendary, which prompted Joe Tait to bellow, "Bingo!" on his radio broadcasts.

Smith earned the nickname before he came to Cleveland. While in college, there were two other Bobby Smiths playing college basketball in Oklahoma at the time.

He came to the Cavs in the NBA's expansion draft on May 11, 1970. He played for the San Diego Rockets during his rookie year after being the sixth overall pick in the 1969 draft. The 6'5", 195-pound swingman played 10 seasons with the Cavs. His 720 games played are third in franchise history behind Zydrunas Ilgauskas (771) and Danny Ferry (723).

When he first came to the Cavs, he drew the ire of coach Bill Fitch. "He called him 'Red Pop,'" *Cleveland Plain Dealer* beat writer Burt Graeff said. It was a popular soft drink at the time, and Smith seemingly drank it by the gallon. "He was in horrible shape [when he came to the team]," Graeff said. "Fitch made a halfway decent player out of him."

Fitch demanded that Smith play defense, something no coach had ever made him do. He became a good defensive player. One thing no one had to worry about was his offensive prowess. He was sixth in franchise history in points scored with 9,513. He averaged 13.2 points in his Cavs' career, including a career-high 15.9 in 1974–1975.

The Cavs retired his No. 7 jersey on December 4, 1979, a little over a month after they traded him to San Diego.

46 The Czar of the Telestrator

The Cavs needed to find a strong coach to replace Hall of Famer Lenny Wilkens after he resigned following the 1992–1993 season. That man was former Atlanta Hawks coach Mike Fratello. He came to the team after several years in the broadcast booth with play-by-play man Marv Albert. He'll be forever known as the "Czar of the Telestrator."

Fratello was hired on June 17, 1993. He helped the Cavs to the playoffs for the third consecutive season, but they were quickly dispatched by the Chicago Bulls in the first round, three games to none. That was the Cavs' final season at Richfield Coliseum. They were moving downtown to Gund Arena for the start of the 1994–1995 season.

Other changes were already underway. Fratello closed practices to the media. He also put a stop to the media traveling on the Cavs' plane. After practice, he didn't want the media talking to players unless they put in a request with the PR department. He was asserting his authority and limiting access to the players.

In the past under Wilkens, practices were open. He had an agreement with the media that certain things weren't going to be reported. There was increased paranoia with Fratello, who didn't seem to trust the media—even though he was part of it for years at NBC. Some say Fratello was influenced by his buddy, New York Knicks coach Pat Riley, who was instituting many of the same access rules in the Big Apple.

The traveling beat writers sat on press row on the court, right next to the Cavs' bench at Gund Arena. After one game, Fratello took Gerald Wilkins out of the game, much to the dismay of the veteran guard. "They were lipping back and forth," *Cleveland Plain Dealer* beat writer Burt Graeff said. "I mentioned it in my story. Fratello got pissed. 'That was a private discussion,' Fratello said. 'There will be a time when you're no longer sitting on the floor.'"

Fratello was certainly right about that, even though he was a little ahead of his time. The Cavs moved the media off the floor when Danny Ferry became general manager in 2005. They were moved up into the second section.

Fratello, a hard-nosed former football player at Montclair (New Jersey) State College, was one of the winningest coaches in NBA history. He ended his coaching career with a 667–548 win-loss record (.549). He coached six seasons in Cleveland and compiled a 248–212 mark (.539). Four of his teams advanced to the playoffs, but he had a lackluster 2–12 postseason record with the Cavs.

Fratello surrounded himself with a strong assistant coaching staff, including Ron Rothstein, Sidney Lowe, Jim Boylan, Marc Iavaroni, and Richie Adubato. All of them went on to become NBA head coaches. "He relied on those guys," Graeff said.

Unfortunately, he came aboard at the tail end of the Brad Daugherty, Larry Nance, John "Hot Rod" Williams, and Mark Price era. They were at the end of their careers. They ended up trading Williams and Price for high draft picks. The Cavs were trying to retool their roster, and still be competitive. Fratello got the most out of a marginal roster.

He tried to control every facet of the game. He wanted to call every play. They drafted Florida State combo guard Bob Sura with the 17th overall pick in 1995. Sura complained that every time he'd make a mistake during his rookie year, Fratello would yank him out of the game. Sura wasn't afraid to say what was on his mind. He told me it was very difficult to play with one eye on the court and the other on the Cleveland bench.

After I wrote the story, I covered practice the next day at Gund Arena. While waiting outside the fourth-floor practice court, Fratello met with the media. While he was talking, I noticed he had a clipboard in his hands. Upon further review, he had my Sura story with certain quotes underlined with a yellow highlighter on the clipboard.

I knew the wrath of Fratello was coming. He waited until all the TV and radio guys left, along with most of the print media. Then he jumped on me about the story. "I can't have stories like this," he said. "It's hard to coach the team with this kind of stuff."

Joe Menzer, my predecessor at the *News-Herald*, told me before he left for the *Winston-Salem Journal* that Fratello was going to test me. He told me, "You have to stand up to him." That's easier said than done. Fratello had a temper. You didn't want to get in his cross-hairs. I tried to stand my ground.

Another time, he wanted to talk to me about something I had written. I was summoned into his office off the locker room by one of the PR guys. I knocked on the door. He told me to come in, but when I got into his office, he was in the shower. We had a discussion about my story while he was shampooing his hair.

Fratello, an immaculate dresser, was the first coach I covered on a full-time basis. To this day, Fratello remains a friend, and I greet him warmly when I see him.

47 The Underappreciated Coach of the Year

Mike Brown was named winner of the Red Auerbach Trophy as NBA Coach of the Year on April 20, 2009. Yet he rarely got any credit for winning the award or being one of the top coaches—percentage-wise—in franchise history. The Cavs' Bill Fitch also won the Coach of the Year award for the 1975–1976 season.

No matter what Brown accomplished, skeptics said it was because he had LeBron James on his roster. There might be some truth to that, but Brown certainly had something to do with it. He was credited with being a good defensive coach, but critics say his offense lacked ingenuity.

Brown guided the Cavs to a franchise-best 66–16 record in 2008–2009 (.805), the best in the NBA that year. The Cavs became just the 12th team in NBA history to win 66 or more games in a season. They had a chance at tying the Boston Celtics' all-time record of 40–1 at home during the 1985–1986 season (37–1 at Boston Garden, 3–0 at the Harford, Connecticut, Civic Center). Brown, though, decided to rest many of his front-line players for the play-offs in their last home game, April 15, 2009, a 111–110 overtime loss to Philadelphia. The Cavs' 27–14 road record (.659) tied for second-best in the league that season.

"Mike Brown is one of these rare people who has nearly every tool in his tool box," Cavs owner Dan Gilbert said. "He is smart, hardworking, and selfless. He is curious and hungry to learn. He is philosophically driven and derives his decision-making from his strong philosophy. Mike is a man of character and integrity. He is a natural leader and has a magnetic charisma, which automatically

Cavs' Winningest Coaches

Coach	Seasons	Record	Pct.
David Blatt	2014–2016	83–40	.675
Tyronn Lue	2016–	27–14	.659
Mike Brown	2005–2010, 2013–2014	305–187	.620
Lenny Wilkens	1986–1993	316–258	.551
Mike Fratello	1993–1999	248–212	.539
Paul Silas	2003–2005	69–77	.473

attracts people to him and his message. He has stuck to his defense-first strategy when it would have been much easier not to. As a human being, Mike treats everyone with respect no matter who they are or where they come from."

Gilbert said Brown was one of the reasons the Cavs continued to grow in stature and success. "I believe I speak for the entire Cleveland Cavaliers organization, from players to Mike's staff to our front office, from the business side and the people that work the games themselves, in conveying how excited and thrilled we are for Mike Brown and his family that he has been awarded Coach of the Year," he said. "There is no man more deserving, and it proves to the world that, yes, nice guys can indeed finish first."

48 Irving Thumbs Nose at NBA Rumor Mill

Despite rumors to the contrary, Cavs guard Kyrie Irving insists he never wanted to be anywhere else. He was mad as hell and not going to put up with it anymore. The Cavaliers guard reacted angrily to a post on the blog *Cavs: The Blog* from April 4, 2014 by Robert Attenweiler, who spoke to ESPN.com's Brian Windhorst. Windhorst once again said Irving's camp has been telling people he doesn't want to be in Cleveland.

Irving responded with a series of tweets, starting with this one: "Sick to my stomach with all these rumors and accusations. Can I play without media guessing at my life and putting B.S out for headlines."

He followed with something that hits home. If someone is going to write or say something as potentially damaging as this, it's proper journalistic protocol to run it by the person. "At least be man or woman enough to come and ask me," Irving tweets. "There's no such source as 'Kyrie's camp.' Nothing but nonsense."

He explained his side of the story before the Charlotte game on April 5, 2014, at Quicken Loans Arena. "It was [in response to] the barrage and attack I saw," he said. "I've been getting it all season. I don't deserve it. It's something that you have to deal with. At a certain point, it's too much. For a third-year player, it's frustrating. No other third-year player has to go through anything close to what I'm going through. I'm not trying to compare myself to anyone else. It got to the point where I needed to say something. It's all bull."

He said he was just tired of all the noise. "'Is he staying or is he going?'" he asked. "That's like the least of my worries right now. It's portraying me in a light and it's bringing negativity to the team that I don't want. Our focus right now, my focus right now, is on winning and trying to finish the season strong."

The stories weren't going to stop until he either accepted a maximum extension in the summer of 2014 or turned it down. "In terms of all the other rumors and accusations, it's been going on all season," Irving said. "It's all nonsense. To go out and portray my character as something I'm not, I'm not an attention-seeker and put those reports out there. To continue to put my name in the headlines to get reads, it's got to stop."

He said those kinds of stories have been there all season—locally and nationally. He got a bit upset when one reporter asked how he felt about the Cavs and Coach Mike Brown. "It's like questions like that," he said. "You're trying to put me in a weird position. I can't

Cavs point guard Kyrie Irving puts up a shot as he gets by the Knicks' Raymond Felton during a loss to New York on January 30, 2014, at Madison Square Garden. Irving had been the subject of rumors all season about whether he would be staying in Cleveland.

say it enough: I love the city of Cleveland, I love my teammates, and my focus is on winning right now."

When the 2013–2014 season ended, the rumors didn't end. However, on the first day of free agency on July 1, 2014, the Cavaliers' front office didn't waste any time. Cavs owner Dan Gilbert, general manager David Griffin, and then new head coach David Blatt and associate head coach Tyronn Lue went to New Jersey to present Irving with a maximum deal. The contract was worth $90 million over five years. It will keep him in a Wine & Gold uniform until 2020. The deal would kick in with the 2015–2016 season.

The Cavs knew they had one factor in their favor. No player has ever turned down a max deal. "We are excited that Kyrie has officially committed to be here long-term with the Cleveland Cavaliers," Gilbert said. "The future has never been brighter as we are building the team and franchise for sustainable success. Kyrie is obviously a very big piece of our plan."

The No. 1 overall pick in the 2011 draft averaged 20.8 points, 6.1 assists, and 3.6 rebounds in 71 games during the 2013–2014 season. Gilbert made Irving the club's top off-season priority—at least until LeBron James let it be known he was interested in returning to the Cavs.

"We couldn't be happier to have Kyrie firmly at the core of our Cavaliers team and family for years to come," Griffin said. "He's already proven he's among the best in the NBA, and we're excited to watch his continued growth and success. To know that he is all-in and shares our high expectations and championship goals is something we're extremely proud of. It is a clear reflection of how we all view our future together, with Kyrie fully vested in this franchise and the city of Cleveland."

Gilbert broke the news on Twitter in the wee hours of July 1: "Looking forward to the next 6 years of Kyrie Irving in CLE," he tweeted. "Just shook hands & intend to sign on the 10th."

Irving quickly followed on Twitter. "I'm here for the long haul Cleveland!!! and I'm ecstatic!! Super excited and blessed to be here and a part of something special. #ClevelandKID."

That ended speculation that he wanted out of Cleveland, and that the Cavs might not even offer him a max deal. Griffin labeled the Cavs' off-season as "monumental." When they were able to sign James, Griffin's comment rang true.

Irving, who called it the best experience of his life, was named 2014 USA Basketball Male Athlete of the Year on December 21, 2014. The USA Basketball board of directors selected the award-winners. "It's truly an honor and a blessing to be among such a great lineage of award winners, and USA Basketball was the best experience of my life thus far, just being a part of a team that's bigger than myself," Irving said. "The sacrifice we all had to make in order to make that team work and the adversity that we faced, and we came home with a gold medal. We were together through it all, and we won a gold medal together, so I'm going to remember it for the rest of my life."

Irving helped Team USA to a 9–0 record in Spain for the FIBA World Cup. He started in all nine games and averaged 12.1 points, 2.6 rebounds, 3.6 assists, and 1.9 steals. The first-place finish qualified the USA for the 2016 Rio de Janeiro Olympic Games. Irving was named MVP after his 26-point, four-assist effort in the gold-medal game. He converted 6-of-6 from the three-point line. "It was a group of guys coming together," Irving said. "People doubted us. We came in there and used that as motivation."

Team USA coach Mike Krzyzewski said Irving came of age during the World Cup. "He's a terrific player, but he became a great player during the summer of 2014," he said. "I think sometimes to become that great player, you need a stage to do it on, and the stage was the World Cup. He performed his best on that stage, and now that's the level he is expected to play at. I'm really proud of him."

A gold medal isn't the only thing Irving brought home with him from Spain. Irving insists he's a much better defensive player. "Kyrie has made progress defensively," Cavs coach David Blatt said. "This summer with USA Basketball helped him mentally and physically."

Irving said he's made a significant step on defense, an area of his game that had been lacking. He started putting intense pressure on the ball, which is the first line of defense. "Coach wants me to do it, and I want to do it," he said. "I actually enjoy doing it. Coach K drew that fire in me and put me out there and told me what to do on the defensive end. It's more or less about trusting the defense and the guys behind me. If I pick up my energy and my defensive pressure, the other guys have to fall in line as well. It's my job as a point guard."

He credits his time with Team USA for honing his defensive skills. His prowess might not result in more steals, however. "Steals can be misleading," Irving said. "If my defensive pressure leads to steals, great. I would trade steals for blocked shots any day. I had three [blocks] in the last game. As long as we get stops and I'm impacting the ball, that's all that matters."

He said playing with Team USA made him a better player. "Playing for two months [in the World Cup] helped me," Irving said. "It put me in a good place as far as my body being in shape. My body feels real good right now."

He earned third-team All-NBA honors in 2014–2015 after having two of the highest-scoring games in the league that season: 57 points versus San Antonio and 55 against Portland. After his record-setting explosion on March 12 in San Antonio, TNT analyst Charles Barkley was left in awe. "This is one of the best individual performances I've ever seen," Barkley said. "He is making tough shots. It's not like he's been wide open." The most impressive shot came at the end of regulation when Irving pulled up for a game-tying three-pointer at the buzzer over the outstretched hand of Spurs forward Kawhi Leonard. That clutch shot tied the score at 110.

Once the teams got into overtime, the Spurs had no answer for Irving (11 points) and Cavaliers forward LeBron James (seven). The Cavaliers rolled to an impressive 128–125 victory over the defending NBA-champion Spurs.

The 57 points were a franchise record and the most scored in the NBA that season. It also matched Golden State swingman Purvis Short's 1984 mark for the most points ever scored against the Spurs. Irving said he loved sharing the moment with James, whom he said shifted into "overdrive" in overtime. "It was awesome," Irving told reporters after the San Antonio game. "It was such a great game. LeBron was hitting step-back threes. We were looking at each other and thinking, *Man, this is so much fun.* This is one of those games where you look back on it as a competitor and you want to be a part of it."

James sure looks like he knew what he was doing coming to the Cavaliers in the off-season in free agency. "The kid is special," he said. "We all know it. We all see it. For him to go out and put on a performance like he did tonight was incredible."

James wasn't too bad, either, as he tallied 31 points. The two All-Stars combined for 88 points on the night. Irving was a career-high 20-of-32 from the field, 7-of-7 from the three-point arc and 10-of-10 from the foul line. "Kyrie Irving was unstoppable," Spurs coach Gregg Popovich said. "I don't know how to guard that. He did a hell of a job. We all know how talented he is, but he really went to a new level tonight. He had a hell of a night and that talent just got us."

James said when one of his teammates gets hot, they feed him the ball. "[Irving] had it going all game," he said. "When you have a guy like that who has a hot hand, you figure out a way, find a way, to get him the ball every time down if need be. You're playing with a guy who's special. It's great to have him on your side. I don't take that for granted."

Irving has a huge admirer in Philadelphia 76ers coach Brett Brown, who coached the former's father, Drederick, in Australia.

"I remember when Kyrie was born," Brown said. "Dred was a New York City playground scorer who could score at will. He was a George Gervin–type player, with his smoothness. He could score in his sleep."

Kyrie said Brown watched him grow up. He first saw Kyrie when he was just a few days old. "The main reason I wanted to play for the Australian national team was because of Brett," Kyrie said. Brown said in his biased opinion, Drederick Irving and Kobe Bryant are the two best shooting guards he's ever seen.

49 Cavs Team Shop Is Over the Top

The multimillion dollar, two-story Cavaliers Team Shop opened October 5, 2010. It's located at Quicken Loans Arena, 1 Center Court, Cleveland, next to the box office. The Cavs say it's one of the largest team shops in the NBA. It houses team apparel for the Cavs, Canton Charge of the D-League, Lake Erie Monsters in the American Hockey League, and Cleveland Gladiators in the Arena Football League.

"We are excited to bring a new Team Shop to The Q for Cavaliers and Monsters fans," Cavs majority owner Dan Gilbert said. "There is nobody who deserves the investment of an ownership team more than Cleveland's loyal, hard-working, and supportive fans. Whether it's the Team Shop, The Q, Cleveland Clinic Courts, or any area on or off the court or ice, it is our commitment to deliver the ultimate experience for our fans that is second to none."

The completely renovated Team Shop was expanded from 3,200 to 5,700 square feet and now includes a second-level mezzanine. "Throughout the design process our goal was to create an experience that would be unparalleled in professional sports, to raise the bar and set a new benchmark by which others can use to measure their own success," said Cavs vice chairman Jeff Cohen, who spearheaded the project. "Until now, state-of-the-art point-of-sale technology and merchandising has only been seen in high-end regional malls and retail stores, and we are thrilled to be able to bring this type of first-class product and experience to our fans."

Direct access to the Team Shop is now possible from two new secondary entry points via existing stairwells—from the Huntington Bank Club Level for suite holders and the Level 5 upper concourse—making it no longer necessary to enter only from the main concourse. Among its features are:

- A two-story, jewel-like, radial glass, pop-out storefront, which creates a dramatic marquee sidewalk entrance off East Sixth Street
- A 24-foot, sliding-glass storefront entrance off the main concourse to give arena event-goers visual access and convenient ingress and egress into the Team Shop
- A scaled-down working replica of the arena's huge center-hung video scoreboard, the focal point of the Team Shop, with four 65-inch LCD screens to beam live game video feeds, graphic content, scores, and statistics on game days so fans will not miss any of the action when shopping
- A three-foot LeBron James bobblehead doll that retails for $600

"First and foremost, our goal with the redesign was to connect the elements of our team and brand and an incredible fan experience to the shopping experience," said Len Komoroski, president of the Cavaliers and Quicken Loans Arena. "The look and feel of the team shop creates an environment where our fans feel the action and energy of what's going on inside the arena bowl. The flow and design of the store also provides for a world-class shopping experience that showcases the [merchandise] as the star."

50 Brad Daugherty: The Cavs' Greatest Center

There have been Hall of Famers. There have been multiple All-Stars. Yet none of the big men could compare to University of North Carolina's Brad Daugherty, arguably the best center in Cavaliers' history.

The five-time All-Star averaged 19 points, 9.5 rebounds, and 3.7 assists in his eight seasons in the NBA. The 7′, 263-pounder from Black Mountain, North Carolina, had his jersey retired on March 1, 1997. His back problems severely curtailed his standout career.

The No. 1 pick in the 1986 draft quickly joined elite status among centers in the NBA. Not only could he score in the post and rebound, he was one of the best passing centers of his era. Daugherty joined Ron Harper, Mark Price, and John "Hot Rod" Williams to turn the Cavs into a perennial playoff contender. He remains the only player in franchise history to average at least 20 points and 10 rebounds in the same season. He accomplished the feat in three consecutive seasons, starting in 1990–1991.

The Cavs advanced to the Eastern Conference Finals in 1991–1992. In 17 playoff games that season, he averaged 21.5 points, 10.2 rebounds, 3.4 assists, and 1.0 blocks in 40.4 minutes per game. He shot 52.8 percent from the field. Daugherty recorded 40 points against the New Jersey Nets on April 23.

Just entering the prime of his career at age 28, Daugherty suffered an ill-fated, career-ending herniated lumbar disc in February 1994. He would never again be the same player he was. He remains in the top 10 all-time in field-goal percentage (second), minutes played (second), field goals made and attempted

Cavs center Brad Daugherty dunks over John Paxson of the Chicago Bulls during Game 6 of the 1992 Eastern Conference Finals at Richfield Coliseum. Daugherty only played eight seasons in the NBA (all with Cleveland) but remains in the Cavs' top 10 in career points, rebounds, assists, blocks, steals, and minutes played.

(third), scoring average (fourth), blocked shots and assists (fifth), and steals (10th).

As part of the Cavaliers 30th Anniversary in 1999–2000, Daugherty was unanimously named by 32 members of the Northeast Ohio media to the Cavaliers' All-Time Starting Five. He was the only player to garner all 32 votes.

Hall of Famer Nate Thurmond and future Hall of Famer Shaquille O'Neal both played for the Cavs, but both were on the last legs of their careers.

No-Fly Zone

While flying home from Charlotte on April 23, 1995, the Cavs' team plane ran into some major turbulence. Players said the plane dropped about a thousand feet, which caused a major disturbance among the high-priced passengers.

Many of the players, including John "Hot Rod" Williams, Mark Price, Terrell Brandon, and Danny Ferry, were scared out of their wits. Some of them said they saw their lives flash before their eyes. A few of the players said they went into therapy because of the incident.

None were more frightened than veteran power forward Tyrone Hill. It was the final game of the regular season, and the Cavs were headed to the playoffs. The 6′9″, 240-pound Hill was so shaken up by the flight, he vowed to never fly again. The Cavs were set to open the first round of the playoffs against the Knicks at Madison Square Garden on April 27, 1995. Their team plane left, but Hill wasn't on it. Instead, he hired a limo to drive him to New York City. It had to be a major expense at the time.

Some of his teammates probably considered going with Hill, but didn't want to get fined. Hill had seven points and eight rebounds in

32 minutes of the Cavs' 103–79 loss in Game 1. He grudgingly flew home with the team, but only after Cavs general manager Wayne Embry put his foot down. "We are a team," he said sternly.

It didn't help their fortunes in the playoff series. They lost to the Knicks three games to one.

52 The Cavs' Four-Month Rental of Luol Deng

The Cavaliers washed their hands of free-agent bust Andrew Bynum on January 7, 2014. They dealt him to Chicago in exchange for two-time All-Star forward Luol Deng. Deng seemed like a perfect fit for the Cavs, who had been trying to find a permanent fixture at small forward since LeBron James left in 2010.

However, the Cavs never entered into any kind of serious dialogue with Deng about a contract extension. The Cavs knew he was going to be an unrestricted free agent after the 2013–2014 season when they made the trade. Deng had turned down a three-year, $30 million offer from the Bulls before the trade.

Deng proved to be a four-month rental for the Cavs.

Looking back at the ordeal, one reason the Cavs didn't want to keep Deng long-term might have been that rumors had already surfaced that James was interested in returning to Cleveland. Of course, those rumors became reality in July 2014.

Deng addressed James' possible return in an interview with Yahoo! Sports: "He's a great player," Deng said. "Why wouldn't you look at him? If he wants to come back home, that's great for him and great for this organization. I'm all right with that. I'm here to do what I can do and be Luol Deng."

Deng's uneasiness with the Cavs became very apparent as the season wore on. It became quite clear by season's end he wouldn't re-sign with the team. The Atlanta Hawks were interested in signing Deng in free agency, but maybe they wish they hadn't been. Hawks general manager Danny Ferry was discussing a scouting report on Deng during a conference call with owners of the team and reportedly said the forward "had some African" in him. Ferry expounded, saying, "He says what you want to hear, but behind closed doors, he could be killing you."

Somehow, those comments made their way to the media. Ferry ended up losing his job over it. The report also said Deng treated Cleveland like a pit stop on the road to a better team. He signed with the Miami Heat in the summer of 2014. Strangely enough, he took James' spot in Miami.

53 Andrew Wiggins: What Could Have Been

Cavs fans will always follow the basketball exploits of Andrew Wiggins and wonder what might have been.

The 2015 Rookie of the Year, now one of the Minnesota Timberwolves' cornerstone players, never played a regular-season game with the Cavs. Cleveland made him the No. 1 overall pick in the 2014 NBA Draft, adding Wiggins to their roster of No. 1 overall picks, which already included Kyrie Irving (2011) and Anthony Bennett (2013).

The Cavaliers opted for Wiggins' vast potential over more of a sure thing in Duke forward Jabari Parker. Ever since his high school days at Huntington Prep in West Virginia, where Wiggins was the Naismith High School Player of the Year, his goal was to be the No. 1 pick. "It's like a dream come true," he said. "I've been dreaming of this moment since I was a little kid."

Wiggins, the mercurial swingman from Kansas, spent less than two months with the Cavs before being included in a trade to Minnesota in exchange for Kevin Love. He was drafted on June 26, 2014, and sent to the Timberwolves on August 23. He was packaged along with Bennett and a trade exception to Minnesota. The Cavs sent a 2015 first-round pick to Philadelphia. The 76ers swapped forward Thaddeus Young to the Timberwolves, who sent Luc Mbah a Moute and Alexey Shved to the Sixers.

Wiggins put on quite a display in the Las Vegas summer league, where rumors broke that the Cavs might include him in the Love trade. His father, Mitchell Wiggins, was a former NBA player with Chicago, Houston, and Philadelphia. He was proud of his son, who earned second-team All-America honors in his lone season at Kansas. "For me, it gives me a lot of closure as a parent and former player," Mitchell said. "It's something he's wanted and dreamed about. He made it happen. He wanted to be the No. 1 pick. It was a strong draft class, as everybody knows. There were a lot of great, talented, young players. He wanted to be on top of that class."

Mitchell said he knew his son was special when he brought him to Michael Jordan's camp when he was in high school.

"Is that your son?" Jordan asked.

"Yeah," Mitchell replied.

"He's got a little something," Jordan said.

Mitchell said he started looking at his son differently. He knew he had something special. "The cameras and glare have been in front of him since he was 14," his father said. "Andrew is mature beyond his years. He's comfortable with who he is. He walks the walk. He's always been a kid who listens and tries to do the right thing."

Mitchell talked about his son's high expectations. "He wants to be a Hall of Famer," he said. "Everybody knows he's got talent. You have to put in the work ethic with the talent and make some internal sacrifices."

Wiggins had All-Star potential, but when the Cavaliers landed LeBron James in free agency, the landscape changed. They were now a championship contender and needed to put the right cast around him. James pushed for the Love trade, and grudgingly, the Cavs included Wiggins in the deal.

Wiggins averaged 16.9 points, 4.6 rebounds, and 2.1 assists in 2014–2015 with the Timberwolves. "At the end of the day, no one wanted to see Andrew go," Cavs coach David Blatt said after his team topped the Timberwolves January 31. Wiggins fired in a career-high 33 points against his "former" team.

Would they have loved to keep Wiggins and watch him develop next to the best player in the league? Sure. But, again, it was about winning now. "That was a deal that was made with the idea of what we wanted our roster to look like, with LeBron coming back [and looking at] what we needed," Blatt said. "Andrew Wiggins is already a fine young basketball player and he's going to be a great player. As is Kevin Love, who we brought to the team to play the position and give us the skill set that we were lacking. So I thought that was a good deal all around and one that should have a good feeling for all involved."

Wiggins went right at James in the game.

"He's a great talent, great talent," James said. "He has a very good feel for the game. That's good to see. He was calm, played the game the right way tonight. He made some mental mistakes, but as a rookie you expect that. I think he's grown each month in this season. They've got a good piece."

Love was also impressed with Wiggins. "You can see that he's going to continue to evolve, get better as time goes on," he said. "Being the focal point of their team, I know they're struggling, but he's going to have a lot of opportunities to better his game this year and in the next few years as they grow and get better as a team. You saw tonight a lot of flashes of what he can do, and he's going to continue to get better."

54 The Strange Case of Bill Musselman

Bill Musselman was known as a fiercely intense coach who never seemed to find a way to deal with losing. Of course, coaching the Cavs at the time might not have been the ideal place for him to be.

Cavs owner Ted Stepien hired Musselman to his first NBA head-coaching job in 1980. Musselman ended up coaching the Cavs on two different occasions—for most of 1980–1981 (25–46) and then again at the end of the 1981–1982 season (2–21). He also held various positions in the organization as general manager and player personnel director.

Musselman was later the first coach of the expansion Minnesota Timberwolves from 1989 to 1991. He was probably best known as coach of the Minnesota Golden Gophers when they physically beat up the Ohio State Buckeyes in a Big Ten game during the 1971–1972 season. Buckeyes center Luke Witte was taken off the court on a stretcher and hospitalized. Witte later played for the Cavs.

Before his successful stint at Minnesota, Musselman coached at Ashland College. His 1968–1969 Eagles team allowed an NCAA record-low 33.9 points per game. Burt Graeff, then a reporter for the *Cleveland Press*, noticed the scores of the Ashland games and ventured down to interview the young coach. "I first met him in the '60s," Graeff said. "I kept noticing these scores at Ashland College, like 52–12. He was the most intense guy I've ever seen. He thought they could shut out a team. They were slowing down the games. He was very successful."

Graeff said Musselman was obsessed with winning. Sometimes that led to rash decisions like playing Cavs guard Randy Smith all 48 minutes in the first exhibition game of the season against Detroit. "He was nuts," Graeff said. "He was extremely paranoid. Sometimes when you talked to him, he was in another world. He was an intense, strange dude."

Colleagues said it was a usual occurrence for Cavs' practice to be delayed while Musselman finished a game of racquetball. Musselman obviously was a basketball savant. He knew basketball but made some of the worst trades in NBA history during his tenure with the Cavs.

The players were well aware of Musselman's peculiar behavior. *Akron Beacon Journal* beat writer Larry Pantages said the team had several pranksters on it, and they loved to mess with Musselman. Once, while he was giving his pregame speech, he was pacing back and forth in the locker room at Richfield Coliseum. All of a sudden, he looked down, and there was a dime on the carpet. He bent down in the middle of his speech and put it in his pocket. That didn't go unnoticed by Cavs players John Lambert and Donnie Ford. They decided from then on there would be loose change lying on the floor. It was their inside joke. They watched intently to see if Musselman would pick it up—and he always did.

Another time, while the team was watching game film with a projector and a tripod, someone interrupted the session and told Musselman he had a phone call. He excused himself and left the room. Lambert and Ford, the team's instigators, immediately sprang into action. They took the screen, rolled it up, and stuffed it up into the dropped ceiling. Musselman came back in the room and asked Cavs assistant coach Gerald Oliver to turn on the projector. He said, "Coach, we lost the screen." The coach informed him to point the projector at the wall and proceeded to show the rest of the game film.

His son, Eric, was a high-scoring prep star at Brecksville High School, near Cleveland. One prankster, who called himself "Super Fan," would follow him around and call him, "Musselhead." Eric

Musselman later became an NBA head coach in Sacramento and Golden State. He's now coaching at the University of Nevada, Reno.

Trading Andre Miller

The Cavs had a star in the making in point guard Andre Miller, the eighth overall pick in the 1999 draft. Cleveland had targeted Miller after Indiana Pacers guard Mark Jackson had shredded them in the 1998 playoffs. They needed a big guard, and Miller fit the bill. He became the first Cavs player to lead the league in assists at 10.9 per game in 2001–2002. However, Miller's rookie contract was about to expire. There were hints that he sought a maximum contract. The cash-strapped Cavs had just rid themselves of Shawn Kemp's massive contract and weren't about to go down that road again with Miller.

Miller's agent, Lon Babby, wanted a max deal that would have been worth $84 million. "We felt it would be in the best interests of everybody if the team tried to trade Andre," Babby told *Sports Illustrated.*

On the eve of the 2002 draft, Cavs general manager Jim Paxson had his lieutenants lined up in the war room. He wanted to hear what they had to say about potentially sending Miller to the Los Angeles Clippers for forward Darius Miles. One after the other, scouts, coaches, and front-office staff gave the thumbs-up on the prospective deal. At least until it came to Cavs assistant coach Ron Ekker. He was a bit crusty, but a notoriously straight shooter. "You can't trade Andre Miller for Darius Miles," he was quoted as saying in *Sports Illustrated.*

Miller was a solid player who could score, distribute, and get to the basket. He was absolutely fearless, as one game against Shaquille O'Neal attests. He repeatedly drove to the basket and kept getting his shots swatted by O'Neal. That didn't keep him from attacking the basket.

Miles, on the other hand, was as athletic as any player in the league. He also was a dunker. Miles and Clippers teammate Quinton Richardson pounded their fists on their foreheads in celebration after every one of their dunks. But Miles couldn't make a jump shot and didn't handle the ball very well. He had major holes in his game.

The trade fell apart on draft night. Clippers owner Donald Sterling supposedly nixed the deal. However, the two sides kept talking, and it was consummated on July 30, 2002. The Cavs sent Miller and swingman Bryant Stith to the Clippers for 20-year-old Miles and forward Harold Jamison. Miles had been the Clippers' No. 3 overall pick in the 2000 draft. "Darius is a player who is potentially a very talented player—but *potentially,*" Clippers general manager Elgin Baylor told L.A. reporters. "[Miller] is a proven player. Darius was a reserve. We gave up a reserve who was not a starting player for a player of this stature. So I just think this is a tremendous deal for us. We took their best player. I don't think they got our best player."

Miles averaged 9.1 points in two seasons with the Cavs. They dealt him to Portland on January 21, 2004, for point guard Jeff McInnis and center Ruben Boumtje-Boumtje. Boumtje-Boumtje (pronounced *boom*-shay *boom*-shay) couldn't play a lick, but it was fun saying his name.

56 Delly Plays Himself into State of Exhaustion

The Kyrie Irving–Stephen Curry matchup in the 2015 NBA Finals would have been must-see TV. Of course, that dream matchup went out the window after Game 1 when Irving fractured his knee cap.

That left Cavs guard Matthew Dellavedova with the unenviable task of defending Curry. It was a case of undrafted free agent versus the league's Most Valuable Player. Dellavedova, a native of Australia, more than held his own—at least in the first few games of the series. He credited his pregame ritual of drinking coffee for his early success.

The 6'4", 200-pounder was treated for dehydration and severe cramping at the Cleveland Clinic after Game 3. He was told by doctors he might have to skip his pregame ritual. "It's not a good thing, probably, for your hydration," he said. "In Finals intensity, it's probably a little different than the regular season. You just try to lay it out there. You're just pushing yourself. I think having 20,000 screaming fans is probably a little bit stronger than a cup of coffee."

His never-say-die attitude has earned him major kudos from the game's best player. "Whatever he has in the tank, he's going to give it all," Cavs forward LeBron James said. "If he has to go to dehydration and cramping again, I think he'll do it again. He gives it all to our team. We just try to reciprocate that back to him."

Cavs guard Iman Shumpert is impressed with his backcourt mate. "He dives on the floor every single play," he said. "[He] gets cut in the face, elbowed, scratched, and keeps on fighting. He's a great teammate to have."

Dellavedova swears he doesn't read any of the skepticism that was directed at him in the NBA Finals. "I mean, I don't really pay attention to anything outside of the locker room because none of that stuff really matters," he said. "As for the motivation part, it's the NBA Finals, and if you need to be looking for extra motivation, you probably shouldn't be playing."

Curry scored 19 points in Game 2 at the Oracle Center in Oakland. However, he made just five of 23 shots from the field, two of 15 from the three-point line. He also committed six turnovers. Dellavedova finished with nine points, five rebounds, and three steals. He also hit the game-winning free throws with 10.1 seconds remaining in overtime.

He refused to take any credit for stopping Curry in his tracks. "I think it's just a team defensive cover," he said. "Everybody has to be alert the whole game because if you lose him for a second, he's going to get a good look. Even if you play good defense, he's going to hit some tough shots, so you've just got to keep defending him and just make it as hard as possible."

James spoke about some of Delly's perceived deficiencies. "I think he's unique in his own way," he said. "Obviously, he's a guy that's been counted out his whole life. Probably people have been telling him he's too small, he's not fast enough, can't shoot it [well] enough, can't handle it good enough, and he's beaten the odds so many times. The confidence that we have in him allows him to be confident in himself. He goes out and he just plays his tail off, and when a guy like that does that, he gets great results."

James said Dellavedova's defensive effort on Curry was a sight to see. He said defenders need to keep a body on Curry at all times and make him work for his shots. "[Delly] was spectacular, man," he said. "You make it tough on him, you get a contest, and you live with the results, and I think Delly did that."

Curry didn't want to hear about if he was going to be ready for the challenge in Game 3. "I doubt this will happen again," he said. "One game won't make me lose confidence."

Curry said the Cavs' team defense is among the best in the league. "That's why they are here," he said. "They have talent on that end. They hustle. They are a great defensive team. They've relied on that in the playoffs."

Curry said he'd forget the poor shooting night in a hurry. "You try to leave it on the floor," he said. "We can take control of the series right back in Game 3. We're still confident. We still believe we're going to win the series."

Warriors coach Steve Kerr's team wasn't used to playing the kind of style the Cavs were playing. James was controlling the tempo in the games and preventing Golden State from running and gunning. "Their defense was great," Kerr said. "They deserve a lot of credit with the way they played. It's rarely a track meet at this stage of the playoffs. This is the Finals. It's supposed to be hard. We had a tough night. We have to learn from it. It was a grind-it-out, old-school game."

Defense is the name of the game in the NBA Finals. "Baskets aren't coming easy in this series," Cavs coach David Blatt said. "Our guys are locked in and making multiple efforts on every play. That's the way you have to play against Golden State."

Dellavedova was taken by ambulance to the Clinic after Cleveland's 96–91 victory in Game 3. "Delly, obviously, suffered from some fatigue," Blatt said. "I don't know whether to call it dehydration or something else, but the tank was low, and we're doing everything we can to fill it back up. That's the best way I could describe it for you."

The Cavs guard provided few details about his time in the hospital. "I was there for a little bit, but mainly just to rest up and recover," he said. "We all [took] it pretty easy today just to get our treatment, and we've watched tape and things like that. So, yeah, I'll be ready to go tomorrow."

Blatt said the Cavs would keep a close eye on Dellavedova. "I told [Delly] I was going to limit his minutes, and he said, 'No, you're not,'" Blatt said. "Look, we've got to be realistic and keep our eyes on him and see how he recovers. He emptied the tank last night. Hopefully, in the ensuing 48 hours he's going to be able to catch up and to get back up to par, so to speak, in terms of his body. But he'll be out there, and we'll just monitor how he's doing. I'm not going to come in there with a specific minute restriction, but we'll definitely be conscious of it."

Delly had a postseason career-high 20 points in Game 3. However, he didn't recover from his time in the hospital. He wasn't the same player in Game 4 and appeared to be physically spent. He managed 10 points and four assists, but shot just 3-of-14 from the field and 2-of-9 from behind the arc. He cramped up in the second half.

"He played his heart out, like he always does," Blatt said. "I don't think he was 100 percent, but he gave us 100 percent of what he had."

Curry got a little frisky with Dellavedova, as well. "We want to make it as tough on him as possible," the Warriors star said. "His game plan is to get into you and make you uncomfortable. If you make him uncomfortable the whole game, it might wear him down."

Dellavedova admitted he can be a little annoying. He was asked if he would find himself annoying. "Yeah, I think I would," Dellavedova said. "In college, guys would try all kinds of things to just distract me or get under my skin and things like that."

Curry, meanwhile, picked up the pace, as the Warriors won the final three games to win the series four games to two.

Dellavedova said he didn't try to play any mind games with Curry. "No, I mean, I don't think you get into the head of a guy like that," he said. "He was the MVP for a reason. He's a cool, calm competitor. So I don't think so."

Cavs guard Kyrie Irving said he wasn't surprised by Dellavedova's early success in the series. "The first time I played against him, he commanded my respect," Irving said. "So, once you step into that— I want to call it a ring—with Delly, you better be ready to rumble. So, for anyone that's ready to go, he's ready to go all the time."

During a game against Indiana on March 20, 2015, he actually asked to come out of the game. I found that quite peculiar and looked for him in the locker room afterward. "I got hit in the nuts," Dellavedova said. "Thanks for asking."

His celebrity grew as the season wore on. He was honored with the Delly Burger at B Spot restaurant in Section 125 at The Q. It is comprised of deli meat, along with red peppers and oregano on a burger.

"Does this mean you've arrived?" I asked him.

"I don't know about that," Dellavedova said. "But it is cool."

"How does it taste?"

"I haven't had one yet," he said.

57 The NBA: Not Just a Game

The NBA's new television deal should be a wake-up call to the 450 players in the league, Cavaliers swingman James Jones said. Jones, the Cavaliers' player rep and treasurer of the National Basketball Players Association, said the nine-year, $24 billion deal that takes effect in 2016 should make the players realize their true value.

"This isn't just a sport anymore," he said. "It's a premier league and one of the biggest industries, not just in the United States, but globally. There are 450 guys in this league who will have the privilege of playing this game for a living. The TV deal reflects just how far the game has come and how far our guys have taken the game since its infancy."

The agreement with ABC, TNT, and ESPN will kick in for the 2016–2017 season and run through 2025.

Forward LeBron James signed a two-year $42.1 million deal with the Cavaliers so that he would be eligible for a more lucrative contract starting in 2016. There will be more money available then, since the NBA's basketball-related income (BRI) is expected to increase drastically with the new TV income. "Being a businessman,

I understand the business of this sport," James said. "That had a lot to do with it."

He said he credits former NBA commissioner David Stern for setting this deal in motion. "He built our league," James said. "He built our brand. For us to be able to make a television deal like that for that type of money, it was a lot of his vision."

James wants the league's rank and file to pay more attention to the business side of this deal. "Sometimes guys want money but aren't educated," he said. "Guys want the best deal but are not educated about what's going on. It's 30 owners, but there are 400-plus players. We know we have to do what's best for all the players, but at the same time, guys continue to need to be educated about it so when the negotiation process happens guys aren't just speaking just to be speaking and have no idea what's going on."

Jones said the new TV deal puts more money into the pool. "It's a huge infusion of cash into the BRI pool," he said. "Immediately it increases the amount of money we share as far as salaries and benefits. But there's much more to it. I'm pretty sure there's a lot left to be negotiated and figured out. But it's a great starting point for us as players going forward as far as understanding our value when we sit down to the table."

James said the latest collective bargaining agreement (CBA) was a good deal. "You always want more and give less," he said. "But I think both sides benefited from it as you see in this new TV deal. Both sides continue to grow. But there's some things we would like to see changed as players going forward."

The players and owners now have a 50-50 split in BRI. At one point, the players had 57 percent of the financial pie. "That's not a conversation I'm going to have today," James said. "We gave a lot. The whole thing that went on with the last negotiation process was the owners were telling us they were losing money. There's no way they can sit in front of us and tell us that right now. We continue to see teams selling for billions of dollars. That will not fly with us this time. We have to figure out how to continue to grow the pot and continue to grow the business of the game. That's the No. 1 objective. That should always be the No. 1 objective—how we continue to grow our game. It's one of the most world-renowned games we have in this world, and we have to continue to do that."

James is first vice president of the NBPA. "My responsibility is to just try and protect the players," he said. "At the end of the day we will negotiate. We know it's going to happen at some point because our deal is ending soon. We'd love to do it sooner than later. We don't want to have happen what happened last time when we went to a lockout. [I'll] just use my knowledge about what's going on and use my business savvy that I have and just try to help us out the best way I can."

Jones said he didn't think the players got snookered in the last CBA. "There was a room full of adults on both sides making conscious decisions about the future of our sport and our game," he said. "We struck a deal that was extremely beneficial to the owners and still beneficial to our players. I don't try to pretend that our players didn't benefit from that deal. We still had the ability to play the sport we love for a generous sum. But at the same time, it's not about the money and how much. It's about the value and getting what we feel is equal value. Not fair value, because each person has their own idea of fair, but what we believe is true value for ourselves."

NBPA director Michele Roberts is calling for significant changes in 2017. The current CBA runs through the 2016–2017 season. At that point, both the owners and players can opt out. Roberts wants the players to get a larger share of basketball-related income. She has serious issues with the rookie pay scale, age limit, and the notion that some NBA teams are still losing money. Many thought that issue was the driving force behind the 2011 lockout.

"There would be no money if not for the players," Roberts told *ESPN The Magazine*. "Let's call it what it is. There. Would. Be. No. Money. Thirty more owners can come in, and nothing will change. These guys go? The game will change. So let's stop pretending."

NBA commissioner Adam Silver was quick to respond. "We couldn't disagree more with these statements," Silver said in a prepared statement. "The NBA's success is based on the collective efforts and investments of all of the team owners, the thousands of employees at our teams and arenas, and our extraordinarily talented players. No single group could accomplish this on its own. Nor is there anything unusual or 'un-American' in a unionized industry to have a collective system for paying employees—in fact, that's the norm. The salary cap system, which splits revenues between team owners and players and has been agreed upon by the NBA and the Players Association since 1982, has served as a foundation for the growth of the league and has enabled NBA players to become the highest paid professional athletes in the world. We will address all of these topics and others with the Players Association at the appropriate time."

Cavaliers forward LeBron James said he was not up to speed with Roberts' comments. "Obviously, we'd love to get together before the deadline so we don't have to go through the same thing we went through a few years ago when we had the lockout," he said. "But I can't comment because I don't know what happened in transcript. I don't want to say nothing that I'm not knowledgeable about. But at some point we'd like to start conversations because you don't want to get to a point where the deadline happens and now we're scrambling. Our game is too good. It's too popular. Everyone loves our game all across the world, and we don't want to get to the point where we have to have another lockout."

58 Wrong Airport

The Cavs ended the 1980–1981 season against the Washington Bullets (now Wizards), who played their home games in Landover,

Maryland. Owner Ted Stepien owned Nationwide Insurance and wanted some of the players to meet with clients after the game. Seven or eight players agreed to fulfill their obligation to schmooze with Stepien's clients.

The rest of the team was supposed to fly home. They piled into a bus and were off to the airport. As they were approaching Baltimore-Washington International Airport, forward Kenny Carr yelled out, "This is the wrong goddamn airport!"

Sure enough, trainer Paul Spicuzza had informed the bus driver to go to the wrong airport. They were supposed to fly from Reagan National Airport. Spicuzza, assistant coach Gerald Oliver, and the bus driver went into the airport in search of the United Airlines desk. They wanted them to call the other airport and inform the United reps at the gate that they were on their way and to hold the flight.

Meanwhile, the players were left to their own devices in the bus. Center Kim Hughes talked the players into commandeering the bus. "Can anyone drive this thing?" Hughes asked.

Guard Randy Smith spoke up. "I can," he said, getting behind the wheel.

After much grinding of the gears, he put it in first gear and took off. Unfortunately for the mischievous players, it stalled. Smith tried unsuccessfully to get the bus started, just as the trainer, assistant coach, and bus driver returned.

They finally made their way to Reagan National Airport and found the rest of the team waiting at the United Airlines gate. The airline now had a dilemma. It only had seven or eight spots remaining on the flight to Cleveland. The players started arguing about who deserved to return on the early flight—the original traveling party or the players who had stayed to party with clients.

Coach Don Delaney had seen enough of the bickering and invited *Akron Beacon Journal* beat writer Larry Pantages to dinner. They returned to Cleveland on a later flight, along with several players that had lost the argument.

59 Cavs' Sneak Peek at LeBron

In the summer of 2002, after his junior year at St. Vincent–St. Mary High School in Akron, LeBron James ventured up to Gund Arena for a workout. On hand were several Cavs players, a few other NBA players, and some local college stars. James, then a 17-year-old prodigy, more than held his own against the competition.

His dunk over Cavs forward Bryant Stith was the talk of the workout. Cavs coach John Lucas attended the workout and came away impressed. The franchise's infatuation with James might have intensified that day.

From that point on, the goal was to land the dazzling prep star from nearby Akron.

The NBA frowned on Lucas' involvement with the workout. It fined the Cavs $150,000 and suspended Lucas for the first two games of the 2002–2003 season. Lucas never made it through that season in Cleveland. He was fired with 40 games remaining and replaced by interim coach Keith Smart.

Century 21 Fan?

One day during the 2002–2003 season, Cavaliers guard Smush Parker called the team and informed coach John Lucas he was going to be late for practice.

Lucas was flummoxed when he spoke to the rookie guard from Fordham. He said Parker couldn't make it on time for practice because he was meeting with his real estate agent.

"I told him if he didn't get here for practice, he wasn't going to need a real estate agent," Lucas said.

LeBron James, a 17-year-old junior for the St. Vincent–St. Mary Irish, drives to the basket in a high school game on March 13, 2002, at Gund Arena in Cleveland. That summer, James would return to Gund Arena in a now-famous workout with several NBA and college players and then Cavs coach John Lucas.

60 Earl Boykins: Small in Size, Huge in Stature

Native Clevelander Earl Boykins, all 5′5″, 135 pounds of him, was the second-shortest player in NBA history. Only the 5′3″ Muggsy Bogues was shorter.

Despite his size, though, "Little Earl" reportedly was able to bench press more than 300 pounds. Boykins averaged 8.9 points and 3.2 assists in 13 NBA seasons. He played for 10 different teams, including two stints with his hometown Cavs—in 1998–1999 and 1999–2000.

"I know I'm different," Boykins told the *Los Angeles Times*. "I know I'll never blend in, but I like who I am. When I think about my height, I think I have really been blessed."

He said his lack of height made him work harder than almost everyone else. "If I was taller, I probably wouldn't have worked as hard or gotten as far," he said. "It's always the same: the first time somebody sees me, they don't think I can do anything. But once they see me [play], then they believe."

It started at Central Catholic High School where he was one of the highest scorers in the Cleveland area. It continued at Eastern Michigan where he turned into perhaps the Mid-American Conference's best player. Yet, when the 1998 draft came, he was ignored by every NBA team. Scouts just couldn't get past his height. It wasn't because he couldn't score. He was forced to play point guard because of his size. However, his game resembled that of a shooting guard. "It was awful, sitting there all day, nobody wanting you," Boykins said of draft day. "After going through that, I think, *How bad can it get?*"

His father, Willie Williams, was a Cleveland police officer. "He told me, 'The only thing that happened today is you didn't get your name called on television,'" Boykins said. "'That doesn't change you or your ability.'"

61 "Best Point Guard in the NBA"

Terrell Brandon was named by *Sports Illustrated* as "The Best Point Guard in the NBA" on February 10, 1997.

He was arguably one of the top 10 point guards in the league at the time of the story. But no one ever confused Brandon with players like John Stockton, Gary Payton, Jason Kidd, or even Allen Iverson.

Sports Illustrated ranked each point guard by their averages in comparison to other lead guards—Iverson was ranked first in points, Stockton second in assists, Kidd tops in rebounds, and Brandon had the fewest turnovers—and tallied up all the results. As Kelly Dwyer wrote for Yahoo! Sports, *SI* added that Brandon was a "sweet guy, and just 5'11"," and somehow fashioned that into a cover story.

But facts are facts. The numbers said he was anything but the best point guard in the league. He averaged a career-high 19.5 points, 6.3 assists, and shot 90.2 percent from the foul line in 1996–1997, his final season with the Cavs. The Cavs finished 42–40 that season. The two-time All-Star was a standout player, but not one of the best in the league.

Brandon, the 11th overall pick by the Cavs in the 1991 NBA Draft from Oregon, played six seasons in Cleveland. He served as Mark Price's backup his first three seasons. Brandon was included in the three-team Shawn Kemp trade. He was shipped to Milwaukee in 1997—seven months after the *SI* story hit the newsstands.

The Cavs' good (but not great) point guard Terrell Brandon looks to pass as he goes by the Nets' Shawn Bradley (45) during a game on January 28, 1997, in New Jersey.

The 5'11", 180-pounder also played for Minnesota before his career was curtailed after having microfracture surgery on his knee. He retired on March 9, 2004, while technically being a member of the Atlanta Hawks—two years after playing his last game with the Timberwolves. He was on the Hawks' roster strictly for salary-cap reasons.

Brandon is owner of the Terrell Brandon Barber Shop in Portland.

62 The Traveling Man

With Chucky Brown, the question isn't whom he played for in the NBA. It was far more appropriate to ask whom he didn't play for.

No NBA player played for more teams than Brown, a second-round pick of the Cavs in 1989 from North Carolina State. The forward played for an NBA-record 12 teams, which tied Tony Massenburg, Joe Smith, and Jim Jackson as the most traveled players in NBA history. All but Massenburg played for the Cavs.

Brown, a 13-year veteran, played in 694 games in his career. It included two stints in Cleveland—nine years apart. He also played for the Los Angeles Lakers, New Jersey, Dallas, Houston, Phoenix, Milwaukee, Atlanta, Charlotte, San Antonio, Golden State, and Sacramento. Brown played 18 games for the Kings during the 2001–2002 season, which signaled the end of his NBA career.

"I am the most traveled man in the NBA," Brown said. The journeyman won an NBA title with the Rockets and a CBA crown with the Yakima Sun Kings in 1995.

63 Don Delaney's Meteoric Rise

When Ted Stepien purchased the Cavs, one of his first moves was to hire Don Delaney. Delaney was astonished when he was approached by Stepien, who bought 37 percent of the team for $2 million from Joe Zingale in the summer of 1980.

Delaney didn't start with an entry-level position. Stepien named him the team's general manager. He had been the men's basketball coach at Lakeland Community College and Dyke College, and earlier at Kirtland (Ohio) High School. He was also the manager of Stepien's professional softball team, the Competitors.

That's not exactly a normal blueprint to run an NBA franchise. But that was the kind of moves the zany Stepien made. To add to this absurd story, Delaney would later become the Cavs' head coach. Coach Bill Musselman started the 1980-81 season—Stepien's first year as owner—by compiling a 25–46 record. Delaney came down from the front office and replaced Musselman for the last 11 games (3–8).

Delaney signed a one-year deal to be the head coach in March 1981. He lasted just 15 games (4–11) before getting the ax. The Cavs had four coaches that season: Delaney, Bob Kloppenburg (0–3), Chuck Daly (9–32), and, once again, Musselman (2–21).

Delaney's 7–19 lifetime record (.269) was one of the worst in franchise history. *Basketball Digest* named Delaney one of the five worst coaches in NBA history. He was an assistant coach with the team in 1982–1983. He served as Cavs' GM from 1980 to 1983.

Delaney died on February 16, 2011, at the age of 75.

64 "Boobie" Goes Off on Pistons

June 2, 2007, will always live in the hearts of Cleveland fans. That was the day rookie guard Daniel "Boobie" Gibson barged his way into Cleveland sports lore with his 31-point effort in Game 6 of the Eastern Conference Finals. He helped the Cavs eliminate the hated Detroit Pistons 98–82 and advance to the NBA Finals for the first time in franchise history. Gibson outscored the Pistons in the fourth quarter of that game 19–16.

The University of Texas product drilled a trio of three-pointers in the first two minutes, 16 seconds of the fourth quarter. When he connected on another long-range shot with 6:52 remaining, it set off a wild celebration inside Quicken Loans Arena.

"If I'm dreaming," Gibson said, "please don't wake me up."

Detroit was making its fifth consecutive appearance in the Eastern Finals and led Cleveland two games to none before the Cavs won the next four games to win the series. The 1971 Baltimore

Bullets and 1993 Chicago Bulls were the only other NBA teams to come back from a 0–2 deficit in the Conference Finals.

Coach Mike Brown spoke highly of the Cavs' second-round pick from Texas. "Boobie is a guy with a lot of poise and a lot of heart," he said during the trophy presentation. "[If] you leave him alone, you better watch out, because it's, 'Boobie for three.'"

Gibson's offensive barrage came one game after LeBron James scorched the Pistons with 48 points in Game 5. "We said we were going to make somebody else beat us, and the kid scored 30," Pistons guard Chauncey Billups said.

Gibson came to the Cavs in the 2006 draft, but only after they ill-advisedly took Michigan State combo guard Shannon Brown in the first round. Gibson moved into Coach Brown's rotation because he could do one thing: shoot the rock. The 6'2", 200-pounder worked out for the Cavs before the draft and then went into hibernation. Other teams hinted that the Cavs "stashed" him to keep them from getting a look at him. The rumor mill said the Cavs gave Gibson a promise they'd draft him with the 42nd overall pick.

Gibson spent seven seasons in the NBA, all with Cleveland, and became a fan favorite. He shot better from the three-point arc (40.7 percent) than he did from the field (40.2 percent). He married R&B singer Keyshia Cole in May 2011. They starred on the BET reality show *Keyshia and Daniel: Family First.*

65 How Baron Davis Trade Reshaped Cavs

Cavs general manager Chris Grant is an easy target. He gets blamed for a lot that went wrong with the franchise in the four years LeBron James spent in Miami. The Cavs had the worst overall record in the league during that four-year stretch.

But one thing on the positive side of the ledger as far as Grant is concerned happened on February 24, 2011. Guard Mo Williams and forward Jamario Moon were sent to the Los Angeles Clippers for Baron Davis and a 2011 first-round draft pick.

Taking on Davis' bloated $13.9 million salary was a bit controversial for the Cavs. Davis was at the end of his career, his knees were like Swiss cheese, and he had a bulging disk in his back. Other than that, everything was fine. Frankly, he was an opinionated player who spoke his mind and sometimes undermined coaches. Davis' career in Cleveland consisted of 15 games during the 2010–2011 season.

The five-month NBA lockout was lifted on December 8, 2011. One of the quirks in the new collective bargaining agreement was the amnesty provision. It was a one-time-only provision that allowed teams to waive a player and get immediate salary-cap and luxury-tax relief. Teams would still have to pay the player his salary.

The provision appeared to be made exactly for a player like the 32-year-old Davis. They would dump the $30 million he was owed over the last two seasons on his contract. He was officially waived on December 14, 2011. That was crucial in getting the franchise back on its feet. It would give them needed cap space moving forward.

As important as eradicating Davis' massive contract was, the actual deal with the Clippers was even bigger. Grant was able to negotiate an unprotected first-round pick in the trade. Clippers GM Neil Olshey took a lot of heat for not putting any protection on the draft pick. The Clippers went into the draft lottery that year with the eighth-best chance at the No. 1 overall pick. After the Ping-Pong balls fell, the Cavs ended up with the first selection.

They drafted Duke point guard Kyrie Irving, which helped the Cavs back on the road to respectability. And, they have Grant to thank for it.

Bagley & Magley Show

Legend has it that Cavs owner Ted Stepien asserted his influence and asked his basketball people to draft Kansas forward David Magley in the second round of the 1982 draft. According to folklore, the biggest reason he wanted him was because his last name rhymed with their first-round pick that year, John Bagley. The Boston College point guard was the 12th overall pick.

Stepien thought the Cavs could market "Bagley and Magley" on the same team.

Magley proved to be a total draft bust. He appeared in 14 games with the Cavs and averaged 0.9 points. He didn't even make it through his rookie year. He was waived in January. Magley later became the commissioner of the National Basketball League of Canada.

Bagley, on the other hand, was a decent player. He played 11 seasons in the NBA, including his first five with the Cavs, and averaged 8.7 points and 6.0 assists. The 6′ guard was fifth in the NBA in assists in 1984–1985 with 8.6 per game.

The Vampire

Edgar Jones played just two seasons with the Cavs, yet he certainly left his mark on the franchise. The guy was out there. He would say about anything. He was also missing most, if not all, of his front teeth. That led to his nickname: "the Vampire."

Jones, a 6'10", 225-pound forward, played six seasons in the NBA. After he was waived by the Cavs in 1986, it marked the end of his career. He showed some promise in 1984–1985 and 1985–1986. Jones would look like an All-Star one night and like the vagabond he was the next. There was no consistency to his game. It seemed like he was injured the whole time he was with the Cavs.

Once, when Cavs trainer Gary Briggs told him he might need arthroscopic surgery to figure out what the problem was, Jones was in the lineup the next night. After signing his letter of intent upon high school graduation, he showed up in the office of University of Nevada, Las Vegas coach Jerry Tarkanian. The Shark didn't know who he was. It was at that point Jones realized he had signed with University of Nevada, Reno.

It was an honest mistake.

"They're both gambling towns," Jones later said.

Once the Cavs hired coach Lenny Wilkens and GM Wayne Embry, Jones' days were numbered. He was waived in the 1986 training camp.

No Dunk Contest for LeBron

The sponsors wanted him.

The league wanted him.

The fans wanted him.

Unfortunately, LeBron James didn't want to participate in the slam dunk contest. The thinking was he's not really an innovative dunker. He's more of a power dunker. Perhaps his management team thought it would hurt his brand if he entered the contest and didn't win.

James doesn't deal well with second place.

During his rookie year in 2003–2004, reporters asked James almost on a daily basis what his plans were for the dunk contest. One day after practice on the fourth floor at Quicken Loans Arena, I asked James, "Are you going to compete in the dunk contest?"

His stock answer, which he gave, was, "I'm not sure yet."

Something happened. I had a momentary lapse in judgment. There was a malfunction with my internal filter.

"Why the hell not?" I asked.

There was silence.

What did I just do?

There was a pause. He looked at me and smiled. It probably shocked him as much as it did me. He reiterated that he just wasn't sure yet. He said he'd let us know when he made up his mind. Of course, that time never came.

It was right around this time the media was writing that James couldn't hit a three-point shot to save his soul. The players and coaches would almost always say they didn't read the stories written about them, but we knew differently.

After a game in Minnesota where James connected on something like five three-pointers, he stopped by press row on his way to the locker room at the Target Center. "Keep writing that shit about me not making three-pointers," he said. He often looked for things to get fired up about, and this was the latest topic.

69 The Transformation of Cedric Henderson

The Cavs had four players in the NBA's Rookie Challenge during All-Star weekend in 1998. The rookie sensations were Derek Anderson, Brevin Knight, Zydrunas Ilgauskas, and the unheralded

Cedric Henderson of the University of Memphis. Henderson was a shrewd second-round pick in the 1997 draft—44th overall—with little or no guarantee of even making the team.

Henderson ended up starting 71 games at small forward for the Cavs as a rookie. Henderson averaged 10.1 points and 4.0 rebounds. He used his uncanny athleticism to run the floor and finish on the break. The 6'7", 215-pounder didn't try to do too much and played within his role.

Henderson was making the league minimum and was a great value to the team. In the summer of 1999, the Cavs signed him to a multiyear deal. He earned $2.4 million for the 1999–2000 season—a financial windfall for the Memphis, Tennessee, native. Insiders say, once he received his money, he was never the same. He became a different player—moody and sullen. The enthusiasm that helped him find an NBA home was gone. The Cavs eventually benched him. When the media converged on Henderson, he said he didn't care.

"Why?" one reporter asked.

"The 15th and the 30th," he replied.

Those were the days NBA players got paid.

Henderson was traded to Philadelphia in the summer of 2001. His five-year NBA career ended later that season.

70 Tanking the 2002–2003 Season

The Cavs were desperate to get their hands on LeBron James. They made sure they were going to be terrible during the 2002–2003 season with a series of peculiar moves in the off-season. Their plan was to tank the season in order to land James in the 2003 NBA Draft. Their ploy worked, as they got the No. 1 pick.

The odd moves started at point guard. They dealt point guard Andre Miller to the Los Angeles Clippers in a lopsided trade that landed Darius Miles. Miller became the first player in franchise history to lead the league in assists during the 2001–2002 season. He averaged 10.9 assists per game.

They waived veteran point guard Anthony Johnson in the preseason and replaced him with marginal talent. Their point guards were rookie Smush Parker and journeymen Milt Palicio and Bimbo Coles.

The Miller trade wasn't the only lopsided deal. They traded sharpshooter Wesley Person to Memphis for guard Nick Anderson. Anderson never reported to the team and ended up retiring. One of the team's top scorers the year before was grumpy forward Lamond Murray, who was upset with the team for not selling his jerseys in the team shop. The last time anyone checked, there wasn't an overabundance of fans clamoring for Murray's No. 30 jerseys. He was sent to Toronto for forward/center Michael "Yogi" Stewart and two draft picks. Murray, often misunderstood in his three seasons in Cleveland, once complained to the media that no one respects his game. That prompted *Akron Beacon Journal* beat writer Chris Tomasson to reply, "I like your game." He made a friend for life.

Cavs general manager Jim Paxson assembled a young, erratic team made up of rookies Dajuan Wagner (the No. 6 overall pick) and Carlos Boozer (No. 35 overall), and youngsters Ricky Davis, Chris Mihm, DeSagana Diop, and Miles. Their best player, center Zydrunas Ilgauskas, made the Eastern Conference All-Star team.

They won just 17 games that season, tied with Denver for the worst record in the league. John Lucas was in his second season as Cavs coach. He compiled a 37–87 record with the Cavs, including an 8–34 mark in 2002–2003. Some called him a sacrificial lamb. When he was fired by Paxson on January 20, 2003, it marked the last time he would ever be a head coach in the NBA. Interim coach Keith Smart coached the final 40 games with the Cavs.

71 Eric Snow: One Tough Interview

Cavs general manager Jim Paxson talked of acquiring Eric Snow for months. He thought the Canton, Ohio, native would be a perfect complement to LeBron James. Snow was anything but an offensive juggernaut, as his 6.8-point career scoring average would attest. But he was a rugged defender, who was the consummate floor general.

Paxson pulled the trigger on a trade with the Philadelphia 76ers on July 20, 2004. He sent Kevin Ollie and Kedrick Brown to the Sixers for Snow. Many in the media thought Snow was a difficult interview. One described it as hand-to-hand combat. He had no tolerance for dumb questions. After asking him a question, there would be a long pause, and then he'd say, "What do you mean by that?"

Some of the team's beat writers would give up after the initial exchange. I liked to volley back and forth with him. I always thought he had a lot to say, but I was definitely in the minority.

I do know Snow liked to read the papers. I wrote a midseason report card for the *News-Herald* that wasn't very complimentary of Snow. Snow was very good at facilitating. He could run the team, find the open man, and get the ball where it was supposed to go. He just wasn't a good shooter.

Shortly after, I approached him in the locker room after a game.

"What about that third-quarter run?" I asked.

"Offensively challenged," he replied.

I'm thinking, *What did he just say? Maybe he didn't understand my question.*

"You know, they really hurt you guys with their outside shooting," I said.

"Offensively challenged," he repeated.

"What are you talking about?" I asked.

"You said in the paper that I was offensively challenged," he said.

I started laughing. I said, "You read that, huh?"

He didn't like the story. He didn't think he was offensively challenged at all. I let him say his piece and we went on about our business.

Snow was also a bit camera shy, which didn't help matters when his wife of 12 years, DeShawn, was cast as an original member on *Real Housewives of Atlanta* in 2008.

72 Chuck Daly: 93 Days as Coach

Chuck Daly's tenure as Cavaliers coach lasted 93 days. He replaced interim coach Bob Kloppenburg during the turbulent 1981–1982 season after being a successful college coach at Penn and an assistant coach with the Philadelphia 76ers. Daly was hired by the Cavs on December 4, 1981. He signed for two years guaranteed, plus one option year.

Daly, of course, reached unparalleled heights after being unceremoniously dumped by Cavs owner Ted Stepien. He won back-to-back NBA crowns with the Detroit Pistons in 1989 and 1990, leading Detroit to the playoffs every year he was its coach and making it to three NBA Finals appearances. He also captured a gold medal as coach of "the Dream Team" in the 1992 Summer Olympics in Barcelona, Spain. It might have been the best collection of talent in the history of basketball. It boasted a roster that included Michael Jordan, Larry Bird, Magic Johnson, Karl Malone, Scottie Pippen, and Patrick Ewing, among others. Daly was obviously qualified to coach the U.S. Olympic team, but not good enough to coach the lowly Cavs? How absurd.

Cavs Coaches for the 1981–1982 Season

Don Delaney (4–11)
Bob Kloppenburg (0–3)
Chuck Daly (9–32)
Bill Musselman (2–21)

However, in Cleveland Daly compiled a 9–32 record. He never felt comfortable enough to buy a house during his short tenure. He stayed at the "luxurious" Holiday Inn of Richfield. One perk to being coach, however, was that Stepien provided all his top men a brand new Lincoln Continental to drive. As Daly would later find out, the luxury car was on loan and not a gift.

When the ax did fall on March 8, 1982, Daly cleaned out his hotel room, piled all his belongings into the Lincoln, and drove back to Philadelphia. That didn't go over well with Stepien. He devised a plan to recoup his car. On the Cavs' final trip to the City of Brotherly Love that season—on April 2, 1982—Stepien insisted Daly return the car to the Spectrum, home of the 76ers.

The owner asked Cavs trainer Paul Spicuzza to drive the Continental back to Cleveland. Spicuzza asked the *Akron Beacon Journal's* Larry Pantages, one of the team's beat writers, to ride back with him so he wouldn't fall asleep.

73 The 50-Point Man

In the 1970 expansion draft, the Cavaliers selected Chicago Bulls center and former Cincinnati Royal Walt Wesley. In preparation for the draft, coach Bill Fitch had sent his lead assistant coach,

Cavs center Walt Wesley (44), who set a franchise mark of 50 points in a game in 1971, fights for the ball against the Celtics' Hank Finkel in a game on March 2, 1972, at Boston Garden.

Jim Lessig, to the store to buy a box of basketball cards. When he returned, they spread the cards out on the floor and went to work.

Lessig went on to become the commissioner of the Mid-American Conference. Early on in his career, though, he was Fitch's right-hand man. They selected several good players in the expansion draft, starting with Wesley. They also picked Bobby "Bingo" Smith, Butch Beard, Johnny Egan, Len Chappell, and McCoy McLemore. The players they drafted would become the backbone of their team in the next few years.

"We took those bubblegum cards in a shoe box and we used them extensively to make our draft picks—vowing that we would never tell anyone because it would have been embarrassing," Lessig said.

The 6′11″, 220-pound Wesley played all 82 games for the Cavs in 1970–1971 and averaged 17.7 points and 8.7 rebounds, both career highs. Wesley scored a career-high 50 points against the Cincinnati Royals on February 19, 1971. He converted 20 field goals and was 10-of-14 from the free-throw line against his former team. He scored 34 of his 50 points in the second half of the Cavs' win.

The former University of Kansas standout holds the distinction of having the lowest career scoring average for a 50-point scorer. He averaged 8.5 points per game in his 10-year NBA career. Wesley's franchise record stood for 34 years. LeBron James barged his way into the Cavs' record book with his 56-point effort at Toronto on March 20, 2005.

At 20 years, 80 days old, James surpassed the San Francisco Warriors' Rick Barry as the youngest player in NBA history to score 50 or more points in a game. According to the Elias Sports Bureau, Barry was 21 years, 261 days old when he scored 57 points against the New York Knicks on December 14, 1965.

James was upset the Cavs lost to the Raptors, despite his record-setting night. "It's a good achievement," James said, "but I'd rather set it with a win."

It took 44 years before a Cavs player would once again score 50 or more points at home—and it wasn't James. Kyrie Irving scored a career-high 55 points versus Portland on January 28, 2015.

Moving to Toronto?

Cavs fans probably don't realize how close the team came to moving to Toronto. This was long before the Raptors came into existence. The Cavs had hit bottom during the 1981–1982 season. The team was atrocious and finished 15–67. The team went through four coaches that season. Attendance was plummeting.

Despite what Cavs owner Ted Stepien was saying to the Cleveland media, behind the scenes, he was scheming to move the team to Canada. He even held a press conference in Toronto where he unveiled a logo for the "Toronto Towers."

The Stepien Rule

Ted Stepien's treacherous reign as Cavs owner spanned from 1980 to 1983. He almost ran the team into the ground, largely with ill-fated trades in which the Cavs relinquished first-round picks.

The NBA instituted the so-called "Stepien Rule," which banned teams from trading first-round picks in back-to-back years. Under Stepien's guidance, the Cavs had dealt away so many first-round picks, the league wanted to protect teams from themselves.

The Cavs traded picks that turned out to be future Hall of Famer James Worthy (1982), as well as All-Star quality talent like Derek Harper (1983), Sam Perkins (1984), Detlef Schrempf (1985), Roy Tarpley (1986), and Dennis Rodman (1986).

After Stepien and his front office sent several first-round picks to Dallas for marginal talent, the NBA stepped in and froze the Cavs' trading rights. That embargo ended after the 1981–1982 season.

Stepien sold the team to Gordon and George Gund in 1983.

Evidently, Stepien didn't think anyone would find out about the possible move in Cleveland. That very day in the *Cleveland Plain Dealer*, Stepien talked about his intention of keeping the team in town. There was such an uproar, he never followed through on his threat to move the team. Powerful radio talk show host Pete Franklin of WWWE started lambasting the bafoonish behavior of the Cavs owner.

Franklin's producer, Dave Dombrowski, recalled that they got so much material from Stepien's day-to-day actions. "The beauty of it is that all we had to do was play off stuff that actually happened," Dombrowski said. "We didn't have to make up anything."

75 Worst No. 1 Pick Ever?

Pundits say the 2013 NBA Draft might have been one of the weakest ever. Years of college players bolting for the NBA early might have caught up with the college game.

The Cavaliers earned the No. 1 overall pick that year—something they've been apt to do in recent history. They were also awarded the first overall pick in 2011 (Kyrie Irving) and 2014 (Andrew Wiggins).

The 2013 draft was wide open with as many as six or seven players vying for the top spot. Something caught the eye of Cavs general manager Chris Grant, who inexplicably landed on UNLV power forward Anthony Bennett. Others in contention for the top spot were Indiana guard Victor Oladipo, Georgetown forward Otto Porter, Kentucky forward/center Nerlens Noel, and Maryland center Alex Len.

Bennett, a 6'8", 245-pound power forward, was recovering from surgery for a torn labrum. By the time he showed up to training camp, he was out of shape and overweight. Coach Mike Brown later said the forward was asthmatic and suffered from sleep apnea. Anything else that could go wrong, did.

The Canadian native was 20 years old at the start of training camp. When Brown instructed his players to run wind sprints, Bennett spent much of the time throwing up. The sight of him bending over, holding onto his shorts, was a common occurrence.

In the annual Wine & Gold Scrimmage, held at Baldwin Wallace University in Berea, Ohio, Bennett entered the game and was gassed after a couple trips up and down the court. He just wasn't ready for the rigors of the NBA.

"It's hard sitting out the whole summer and trying to come back with the conditioning," he said. "If I drop a couple pounds, it will be helpful. I think I'm at 250 right now, which is about eight pounds heavier than I played in college. I'm pushing myself with all these guys around me."

Bennett worked extremely hard to get into NBA shape. But once the regular season started, things went from bad to worse. He missed his first 16 shots from the field. He tried to keep his spirits up, but it was difficult. He quickly became the butt of many national jokes, and was labeled as a draft bust.

Bennett lasted one season with the Cavaliers. He's been lumped into a list of the worst No. 1 overall draft picks of all-time, joining LaRue Martin (1972, Portland), Greg Oden (2007, Portland), Michael Olowokandi (1998, L.A. Clippers), Kwame Brown (2001, Washington) and Pervis Ellison (1989, Sacramento).

Bennett was included in the Kevin Love trade on August 23, 2014, and spent one unproductive season with the Minnesota Timberwolves in 2014–2015. The two sides agreed on a buyout of his contract on the eve of the 2015 training camp. After becoming an unrestricted free agent, Bennett signed a minimum deal with the Toronto Raptors. He later became the first No. 1 overall pick to play in the NBA Development League (D-League).

76 Cavs Finally Land a Rim Protector

The Cavs went almost five years before they landed a legitimate replacement for Zydrunas Ilgauskas. Since Ilgauskas' retirement—he last played for the Cavs in 2009–2010—Cleveland got by using a cast of imposters.

That ended January 7, 2015, when they sent two protected first-round picks to the Denver Nuggets for Timofy Mozgov. The Cavs admit it was a steep price to pay, but it was necessary with the medical history of Anderson Varejao. Varejao had stepped in after Ilgauskas followed LeBron James to Miami for the 2010–2011 season. Ilgauskas retired after his lone season in South Beach. Varejao, a converted power forward who got by on guile and hustle, suffered a season-ending torn Achilles tendon on December 23, 2014. His injury stepped up the urgency to find a big man.

James said he's played with some very good big players. "You know, Chris Bosh is a great big," he said. "Kevin Love is a great big. But I'm talking about a true seven-foot big guy. [Mozgov is] probably the best one I've played with since Z. They have different skill sets, but they both have skill. They know how to play. Sometimes you get a lot of bigs that are just big. He knows how to play, and it's great to have him out there."

The Cavaliers had been searching for a rim protector for quite some time. It appears as if they found one in the 7'1", 250-pound Mozgov. It's not so much the blocked shots with Mozgov. He's most effective just standing next to a player, utilizing his 86" wingspan. He really understands the rules of verticality.

"If you drive to the basket, you know he's going to be there," James said. "He's going to block a shot, change a shot, or foul you. To have that kind of protection is huge for us."

Like good quarterbacks, rim protectors are hard to find. "Every team would love to have one," James said. "In Miami, we tried to do it collectively. We tried to protect the rim with our speed and quickness. Bird [Chris Andersen] gave us some of that with his effort and energy. To have Timo come out, he raises the level for all of us. If we get beat, which is going to happen with the greatest guys in the world, you are going to have someone at the rim to help you out. He knows how to play."

Mozgov isn't going to sneak up on teams. They are well aware of his presence in the middle. The Cavaliers are funneling their defense to the paint where Mozgov is waiting. "He's going to be on the scouting report," James said. "He's a walking double-double."

Then Cavaliers coach David Blatt had known the native of St. Petersburg, Russia, for years. "He's made himself into a better player," Blatt said. "He's more mature and confident. He's had good coaching and worked very hard. We brought Timo to the Russian national team in 2009. That was his introduction to the worldwide basketball scene. Then he followed up in 2010 with a great performance in the World Championships in Turkey. Then he won a medal in the 2011 European championships and a [bronze] medal in the 2012 Olympics. He just got better and better every year. The player I see now is better than the player I saw then. He's so active. He gets his hands on so many balls, which gains extra possessions for us."

When Cavs general manager David Griffin brought Mozgov to the team, he said he fit their needs in a big way. Truer words have never been spoken. Not only does he anchor their defense, he is the recipient of many alley-oops. The guards just lob the ball toward the rim. He does the rest. "I love to dunk," he said.

Blatt said Mozgov was a factor in the Cavs turning around their 2014–2015 season. "He fits in well with the other guys," he said. "He's a great teammate, well-liked. He's big. You can't teach that."

Yet, on many occasions, Mozgov could be found sitting on the bench in the fourth quarter. Blatt deployed the defensive-minded Tristan Thompson during crunch time.

When Mozgov first came to the team, I was shooting video in the locker room. That consists of me standing next to him, holding the camera straight up toward the ceiling. While editing the video later, I got a good laugh. He looked right at me, smiled, and winked into the camera. It doesn't take much to amuse me. Another time, after a February game against Philadelphia, Mozgov sat in front of his locker with a giant pizza box on his lap. He proceeded to consume the 16-piece, extra-large pizza by himself.

77 Don't Mess with Lonnie

Forward/center Lonnie Shelton was one of the toughest guys to ever play for the Cavs. The 6'8", 265-pounder took pride in setting immovable picks. It was an era in the NBA when players settled their differences on the court.

No one will ever forget the time someone tried to rob him at gunpoint after Shelton and his girlfriend dined at a downtown Cleveland restaurant. Shelton grabbed the gun from the would-be thief, pummeled the guy, and was sitting on him when the police arrived.

Shelton was quoting Bible verses to the man, who replied, "Yes, Mr. Shelton. You are right, Mr. Shelton."

He handed the gun to his girlfriend. "If anybody moves, shoot 'em," he said.

Another time, he got in a fight with Milwaukee Bucks forward Paul Pressey, later an assistant coach with the Cavs. He chased Pressey off the court and into the tunnel that led to the locker rooms at Richfield Coliseum. According to a story in the *Cleveland Plain Dealer*, Shelton screamed at Pressey and said, "I'll end your career!"

Shelton also got into a skirmish with New Jersey Nets forward Buck Williams and chased him into the stands. Williams, a rugged power forward who played 17 seasons in the NBA, wanted nothing to do with Shelton.

"Off the court, Lonnie Shelton was one of the nicest guys to play here," Cavs radio announcer Joe Tait told the *Plain Dealer*.

Shelton played three seasons with the Cavs after being acquired from Seattle for a 1983 second-round pick and cash on June 27, 1983. Shelton's son, L.J., played 10 seasons in the NFL as an offensive tackle, including the 2005 season with the Cleveland Browns.

Lonnie Shelton's 1985–1986 season with the Cavs was his last in the NBA.

78 The Mysterious Case of Chad Kinch

On draft day 1980, Cavaliers coach Stan Albeck went to the podium and announced they had drafted North Carolina–Charlotte guard Chad Kinch. Albeck made the No. 22 selection, and witnesses said he left the premises.

He denied this in the book *Cavs: From Fitch to Fratello*. "I stayed until the end of the draft," he said. "And, yes, I drafted Kinch. I drafted Chad Kinch because I thought he could play." Of course, he couldn't.

Owner Ted Stepien wanted Albeck to draft North Carolina big man Rich Yonakor, a local product from nearby Euclid High School.

"'Look, Ted, he's not good enough to be a No. 1 pick,'" Albeck said he told Stepien. "'Maybe Dean Smith can find him a good job in another field or something.'"

"Who's Dean Smith?" was Stepien's reply, according to Albeck.

Albeck said he knew he was in trouble dealing with Stepien, especially if the owner had never heard of the legendary Tar Heels coach. Bill Musselman, the Cavs' personnel director, made some of the subsequent picks. By the end of the draft, the front office had cleared out.

"By the ninth round, I'm there by myself," Cavs public relations director Bill Needle said. Needle said he drafted Central State shooting guard Melvin Crater with the 187th overall pick.

Needle said he introduced himself to Crater in training camp and informed him that it was he who drafted him in the ninth round. "Oh, yeah, how come so late?" he replied.

Crater never made it out of training camp.

Albeck, though, was long gone by then. He left to coach the San Antonio Spurs the day after the draft. Kinch averaged 2.8 points in 29 games with the Cavs in 1980–1981. He was traded to Dallas during his rookie season.

He died of AIDS-related complications in 1994.

Needle was later fired by Stepien for associating with radio broadcaster Joe Tait on the road. Stepien and Tait had been feuding for the latter's criticism of the team on the air.

79 The Two-by-Four Man

During a game against the Indiana Pacers on January 22, 1992, Cavs guard John Battle claims he got sucker-punched by Indiana forward George McCloud.

After the Cavs put the finishing touches on a 119–115 overtime victory, Battle grabbed a two-by-four from a supply closet in the Richfield Coliseum and went after McCloud. Battle was normally a mild-mannered player, but he just lost it. Luckily for McCloud, Battle didn't catch him.

However, that wasn't the case for a New York writer who came to the Coliseum to cover a Knicks game in the late 1980s. He tried to use a phone already commandeered by radio host Greg Brinda, and an argument ensued. The mild-mannered Brinda didn't mess around. He dropped the writer on the floor in a one-punch fight.

A game against the Boston Celtics didn't escalate that far. While jostling for a loose ball, LeBron James got tangled up with Celtics players Paul Pierce and Kevin Garnett. Some pleasantries were exchanged.

Before anyone knew it, LeBron's mother, Gloria, was in the middle of the fray. Gloria, about 5′ and 100 pounds, was ready to throw down.

James looked at his mother and set her straight.

"Sit your ass down!" he bellowed.

James had carried a long feud with Pierce that stemmed back to the former's rookie year. In a preseason game at Value City Arena at the Schottenstein Center in Columbus, Ohio, Pierce had spit toward the Cleveland bench. As the two teams filed off the court at the end of the game, there was some pushing and shoving. Security kept any punches from being thrown.

The best line after the game had nothing to do with the tussle, however. A Columbus television reporter asked Cavs coach Paul Silas what he thought of the Schott (as in the Schottenstein Center).

"Which one?" Silas replied.

Wild Thing

Anderson Varejao had a built-in theme song, "Wild Thing" by The Troggs. Whenever he entered a game at Quicken Loans Arena, the game operations staff would play the 1966 hit song.

The mop-topped Brazilian was beloved in Cleveland for his incessant floor burns and all-out hustle. No one played harder. The downside was that he was unable to stay healthy. He missed 222 of a possible 394 games during a five-year stretch from 2010 to 2015. Varejao suffered from knee problems, shoulder problems, a torn Achilles tendon, and a blood clot in his lung, among others. He had such total disregard for his body, it was difficult for him to stay in the lineup.

When he's able to remain upright, he's one of the top backup centers in the league. He's not a great scorer, but he rebounds and defends and just knows how to play the game. The Cavaliers have had numerous opportunities to trade the 6'11", 267-pound Varejao over the years. According to a report on ESPN.com, the Los Angeles Lakers offered forward/center Pau Gasol to the Cavaliers in 2014 for the Brazilian big man. Finally, on February 18, 2016, the Cavs traded Wild Thing away in a three-team deal to Portland, who immediately waived him. A week later, Varejao signed with Golden State, where he played the rest of the season, making it to the Finals against his former team, only to be on the wrong side of the court for the second year in a row.

When LeBron James had returned to the team in 2014, he relished the fact that his old running mate was already in place. The two had played together and became quite close during James' first

Cavs backup center Anderson Varejao gets called for a foul against the Houston Rockets in a game on December 2, 2006, in Houston. His hustle and distinctive mop of unruly hair made him a fan favorite during his 12 years in Cleveland.

stint with the Cavaliers. "He's the same Andy," James said. "If you ask him to run through six walls, he'll run through seven.

"He'll fight for every loose ball. He'll dive on the floor. He'll set screens. He'll help you out when you get knocked down. If any altercation happens, Andy will be right there. We just need him to stay healthy."

Varejao never liked to discuss his injuries. He'd rather emphasize the good times. "Let's talk about the healthy years I've had," Varejao said. "I feel good, especially after what I went through."

Some fans would hold their breath every time Varejao hit the deck. They figured it was only a matter of time before he'd get injured.

Being reunited with James was a "great thing," Varejao said. "The last four years, we went through a rebuilding process. It wasn't fun. I had some injuries that I want to forget about. It seems as if everything is new."

He saw a change in James. He's now a seasoned veteran. "He's much more mature," Varejao said. "He's won a couple of championships and went to four straight Finals. The way he works out, the way he does things, the way he comes here every day, he's much more professional. I'm not saying he wasn't before. It's good to have him back. I believe he can help us get to the next level."

Then Cavs coach David Blatt said he'd known Varejao since the latter played for F.C. Barcelona in Spain. Interestingly enough, that's where former Cavs GM Jim Paxson first discovered Varejao. "I've had a lot of contact with him through the years through the international tournaments both of us were involved in, Olympic Games and World Championships," Blatt said. "But being around him every day gives you a sense of what a great person he is and a fine basketball player, and how much he means to Cleveland and the Cleveland community. He's a genuine guy. People respond to genuine people. That's Cleveland to me."

When the Cavs lost Carlos Boozer to free agency in 2004, Paxson was on the prowl for a power forward. He ended up trading for two very good ones. Paxson sent Tony Battie and two second-round picks to the Magic on July 23, 2004, for Varejao, Drew Gooden, and Steven Hunter. Gooden became the Cavs' starting power forward—essentially replacing Boozer—and Hunter was waived before he ever played a game with the team.

Some referred to Varejao as a throw-in to the trade. That proved to be anything but the case. The Cavs handed out Varejao wigs to fans on February 21, 2014. It shattered the Guinness world record for "most people wearing wigs in a single venue." Of course, I had to wear one, even though from all accounts, I looked ridiculous.

81 Walt Frazier: The Epitome of Cool

The New York Knicks' dynasty was starting to crumble. The so-called "Rolls Royce" backcourt of Walt "Clyde" Frazier and Earl Monroe was starting to get old.

Their two NBA championships were in the rearview mirror. The Knicks missed the playoffs for two consecutive seasons, and it was time to rebuild. In compensation for signing guard Jimmy Cleamons in free agency, the Knicks sent Frazier to the Cavs. One of the most glorious careers in Knicks' history came to an end.

At the time of the October 10, 1977, deal, the 6'4", 205-pound Frazier ranked as the Knicks' all-time leader in points (14,617), assists (4,791), games (759), and minutes (28,995). Frazier was stunned by the trade. After a decade in the Manhattan limelight, he reported to Cleveland. He was definitely on the downside of his career when he arrived, even though he had a good first season with the Cavs. He averaged 16.2 points, 4.1 rebounds, and 4.1 assists in 51 games in 1977–1978.

A seven-time All-Defensive Team player, his hands were reputed to be "faster than a lizard's tongue." He earned first-team All-NBA honors four times. He wore fur coats and wide-brimmed hats and drove a Rolls Royce. He practiced yoga long before it became fashionable for pro athletes.

But it all went downhill for Frazier after his first season in Cleveland. The seven-time All-Star played just 15 games over the next two seasons before the Cavs placed him on waivers after three games in the 1979–1980 campaign. That signaled the end of his illustrious NBA career. He became a Knicks' broadcaster after his playing days were over.

Frazier was inducted into the Naismith Memorial Basketball Hall of Fame in 1987 and named to the NBA's 50th Anniversary All-Time Team in 1996. The top 50 players were introduced during All-Star weekend in Cleveland in February 1997. Only three players were not in attendance: the late Pete Maravich, Lakers GM Jerry West, and Lakers center Shaquille O'Neal.

The press conference introducing the all-time greats at a downtown Cleveland hotel was one of the highlights of my career. When I walked into the ballroom, there was Bill Russell at one table, Wilt Chamberlain at another, and George Mikan at yet another. It was unbelievable. It was a Hall of Fame smorgasbord. I was like a kid in a candy store. I couldn't get enough of it.

Almost 20 years later, the Cavs and the Greater Cleveland Sports Commission have made a bid on the 2018 NBA All-Star Game. "[We've worked on it] hand-in-hand," Greater Cleveland Sports Commission president and CEO David Gilbert said. "We've worked very closely on it together. The city of Cleveland was also involved. We've taken the lead."

Gilbert said 2018 was picked because of the availability of Quicken Loans Arena that weekend in February. In the past, available hotel rooms were the big issue with hosting a game of this magnitude. Gilbert said there are now twice as many hotel rooms in downtown Cleveland than there were in 1997, the last time the Cavaliers hosted the game.

"The new infrastructure downtown has elevated our ability to host the game," Gilbert said. He said the NBA needs about 6,000 hotel rooms in close proximity to the downtown area for the game.

The 2016 Republican Convention needs about 16,000 rooms, Gilbert said. He said there will be six new hotels built in the next three years.

Gilbert said he feels good about Cleveland's chances for the All-Star Game. He said he doesn't know what other cities are bidding for the game. Reportedly Portland and Charlotte have also bid on the 2018 game. "We believe very strongly that we'd be a tremendous host," Gilbert said. "We feel very confident."

Cavaliers forward LeBron James said he would be overwhelmed with ticket requests if Cleveland hosted the game. "It would be too much to me," he joked. "I think it would be great for us to host it. Hopefully, I'm no good that year if we get it. I don't want it with family and friends. I don't want it."

82 Cavs Chase Izzo, End Up with Scott

When the Cavs finally offered Byron Scott the head-coaching position in July 2010, some believe he was actually their fourth choice. It started when Mike Brown was unceremoniously dumped after the 2009–2010 season. After back-to-back seasons of 66 and 61 wins, he was shown the door.

Cavs owner Dan Gilbert had an infatuation with Michigan State coach Tom Izzo, a highly successful, in-your-face coach with the Spartans. Gilbert had gotten his undergraduate degree at Michigan State and was convinced Izzo's style would work in the NBA.

We'll never know. Despite making him a reported five-year, $30 million offer, Izzo decided to stay at the East Lansing, Michigan, school. "Instead of coaching them in the NBA, I'm going to coach them in the NCAA," Izzo said at a news conference. He had asked for an audience with Cavs forward LeBron James, who was an unrestricted free agent. That never happened, which helped sway his decision.

"That was one of the key factors, 100 percent true," Izzo said. "That was not the only factor. Was it a big factor? Sure."

Izzo contemplated it for nine days before nixing the Cavs' offer. "I knew at the beginning that whatever decision I made would be a decision for life," Izzo said. "I am going to be a lifer. This is what I'm going to be, and I'm damn proud of it."

Gilbert said it was not to be. "The entire Cleveland Cavaliers organization has nothing but respect and admiration for Coach Izzo and his family," he said in a statement. "Tom is a special person in so many unique and positive ways. We only wish great things for him and his family in all the years ahead."

The Cavs talked to Milwaukee Bucks assistant coach Kelvin Sampson, who quickly fell out of the running. Los Angeles Lakers assistant coach Brian Shaw, former Atlanta Hawks coach Mike Woodson, and ex–New Jersey Nets and New Orleans Hornets coach Scott were also interviewed.

After Shaw's interview, his agent tweeted out several messages from the Cavs headquarters at Cleveland Clinic Courts in Independence. He hinted that Shaw was close to accepting the job. In a peculiar chain of events, Scott's agent, Brian McInerney, sent out a congratulatory message to Shaw. There was only one problem. The Cavs say they never offered the job to Shaw.

Scott, who spent an hour on the phone interviewing with Cavs GM Chris Grant and assistant GM Lance Blanks, was quickly back in the running. Many thought Scott was holding out for his dream job—the Los Angeles Lakers. He ended up accepting the Cavs' job on July 2, 2010—about a week before James made his famous *Decision*. Scott took the job thinking he'd be coaching the best player in the league. Instead, he ended up coaching "immortals" like Samardo Samuels, Christian Eyenga, and Semih Erden.

When Brown was the Cavs coach, much was made about the fact that he never played in the NBA. The Cavs now had a coach with three NBA championship rings with the "Showtime" Lakers, as well as an NBA Coach of the Year honor in New Jersey in 2008. In the end, however, it didn't matter. The Cavs didn't have the talent to compete.

With James heading to South Beach, Scott recorded a 64–166 mark (.386) in his three years as coach—the worst mark in the NBA during that stretch. Scott said later he isn't sure he got a fair shake when he was fired after the 2012–2013 season. He said he thought he'd have until December of the following season to get things straightened out. That time never came, as he was fired on April 18, 2013.

"When it did happen, yeah, I was a little disappointed," he said February 8, 2015. "I think as coaches, when it happens, we're a little disappointed. Most of us feel like you didn't get a fair chance. I guess I'm no different."

He accepted the job without knowing what was going to happen with LeBron James. He was hired on July 2, 2010, and James bolted for Miami eight days later. Scott said it was a gamble worth taking. "I never look back," he said. "I try to focus on the present and the future. The past, I can't do anything about that."

He's now in a similar situation with the Lakers. "It's the same process," Scott said. "We're trying to build a different culture. It's no different than it was in Cleveland two years ago."

Scott said he did enjoy his three seasons with the Cavaliers. "The people were great," he said. "The city was great for me."

Scott said he was a bit surprised that James returned to Cleveland in 2014. Scott heard Heat president Pat Riley's comments about a week before the Decision 2.0 that said players need to have the guts to stay and work things out. Riley said many players just look for a way out when things go awry. "I'm sure LeBron took that as a challenge," Scott said. "He was a free agent. He chose to come back [to

Cleveland]. When I first listened to [Riley], I said, 'Whoa.' I guess LeBron did, too."

Scott's firing in Cleveland touched off a carousel of coaching changes in the next few years surrounding the Cavs and Lakers. In a strange twist of fate, Brown was hired by the Lakers to be their head coach for the 2011–2012 season. He didn't fare much better than Scott. Brown was fired after one full season. After the Lakers got off to a 1–4 start in 2012–2013, he was sent packing.

So what happened after Scott was fired by the Cavs? They rehired Brown for the 2013–2014 season. He lasted one season in his second go-round in Cleveland and was fired again. He'll never have to worry about money the rest of his life. He had a reported three years left on his contract when he got the ax.

Scott was hired by the Lakers—his dream job—for the 2014–2015 season.

Brown was a personable fellow but didn't give up information easily. He just couldn't answer questions like, "How's Zydrunas' ankle?" It wasn't in his makeup. Fellow reporters like Brian Windhorst would chide me for asking.

During his first stint with the team, Brown went out of his way to explain his defensive theories to the media. I asked him once to clarify his "sink-and-fill" concept, and he took the entire media group out onto the practice court and expounded on it thoroughly. In case you wondered, I was manning the "4" spot on defense.

83 The 100-Point Man

Guard Dajuan Wagner set a New Jersey single-game prep record with 100 points for Camden High School on January 16, 2001, in a 157–67 win over Gloucester Township Tech. Of course, it paled in comparison to Wilt Chamberlain's 100-point outburst against the New York Knicks in 1962. Wagner's effort was a remarkable feat, even if it was on the high school level.

However, it would almost haunt him for his entire NBA career. In that game, he was 42-of-60 from the field, 10-of-15 on three-pointers. Wagner went on to set a state career scoring record with 3,462 points.

After one season at Memphis, he entered the 2002 NBA Draft. The Cavs selected him sixth overall. He never lived up to his vast potential. In his first couple years in the NBA, whenever he was mentioned, the writer also referred to Wagner's 100-point game in high school.

I ran into Cavs coach John Lucas the night before the draft at a Cleveland Rockers game. Of course, I questioned him about who the Cavs would draft. He replied, "You should be able to figure it out. It's clear as day." Knowing Lucas played for Maryland, I incorrectly latched onto Terrapins power forward Chris Wilcox. I had heard rumblings that Cavs GM Jim Paxson liked UConn guard Caron Butler.

It all made sense when Wagner's name was called, though. Lucas was a former guard, and was infatuated with Wagner's scoring ability.

But right from the start, the 6'2", 200-pound Wagner couldn't stay healthy. He was compared to the Philadelphia 76ers' mercurial guard Allen Iverson, which wasn't fair to Wagner. Cavs fans did catch a glimpse of what might have been in Wagner's third NBA game. Wagner erupted for 29 points against the Sixers on November 29, 2002. The 76ers prevailed, 106–99, as Iverson also had 29 points.

Wagner's father, Milt, was an NBA guard. "Juannie" averaged 13.4 points during his rookie year, but things went downhill from there. He spent three seasons with the Cavs, and one game with Golden State in 2006–2007 before his NBA career fizzled.

He never developed as an NBA guard. He was the size of a point guard, but couldn't handle the ball well enough to play the position.

He was a shooting guard, but an undersized one. He also didn't have a reliable jump shot, as his .366 career field-goal average attests.

During his second season in the NBA, the Cavs played at Memphis on April 7, 2004, at the Pyramid. While I was walking down a hallway to the Cavs' locker room, Memphis Tigers coach John Calipari was walking with me. He wanted to see one of his prized pupils. The Tigers played their home games at the Pyramid. A security guard stepped out from a desk and said, "I need to see your credential." I stopped and showed him my pass. He totally ignored me and stopped Calipari in his tracks.

"Do you know who this is?" I asked.

As I was entering the locker room, I glanced back down the hall and noticed that Calipari was being escorted out of the building by the overzealous security guard.

A little later, while in the locker room for pregame access, Calipari entered and gave Wagner a warm embrace. While walking back to the press room, I noticed the security guard was no longer at his post. For all I know, he was in the unemployment line.

84 Tristan's Big Change

Cavs power forward Tristan Thompson is one conflicted young man. Many NBA players spend the summer honing their game. He spent the summer of 2013 learning how to shoot right-handed. He made the transition from being a lefty for his entire basketball career up to that point. He entered his third season in the NBA a right-handed shooter. "I'm 22," he said. "I'm trying to figure it out myself."

Now that we know he's a righty—at least for the time being—he revealed he also bowls right-handed. He writes left-handed, along with eating and golfing.

"I'm ambidextrous," he said. "I do a lot with my left and right."
It's the first time this transformation has ever happened at the NBA level, at least as far as anyone can remember. "There's no blueprint," he said.

Cavs swingman C.J. Miles previously told Thompson he ought to shoot right-handed after seeing him make one of his push shots. "C.J. is like a Miss Cleo or something," Thompson joked. "Right now it's more physical than mental. It was something I wanted to do. I wanted to take on that challenge."

He said he originally shot left-handed because of the way he wrote. "I wrote with my left hand, so I thought if you write with your left hand, you have to shoot with your left hand," Thompson said. "If I'd lived in the [United] States and started playing at an earlier age, that transition might have happened sooner. When I started playing in Canada at the age of 12, I had coaches, but they didn't compare to the coaches down here as far as knowledge. If they had said, 'That shot is ugly,' I would have started it sooner."

That's not all he did that summer. He said he worked on getting stronger, ways to be more effective defensively, and to develop as a player. The 6'10", 238-pounder shot 47.7 percent from the field in 2013–2014, his first season as a right-hander. He improved to 54.7 percent in 2014–2015.

Thompson has a big role with the Cavs. He's normally the first big off the bench. Of course, in the Cavs' 2015 playoff run, he moved into the starting lineup when Kevin Love was injured. Thompson operates under the radar. He doesn't get much fanfare. Rarely is he ever in the headlines. Yet he's one of the team's unsung heroes. "I'm bringing the energy," Thompson said. "That's my role on this team. That leads to getting extra possessions on the court. Defensively, just taking on the challenge of guarding the other team's best big and giving Timo [Mozgov] and Kevin a breather."

When he's competing against players bigger than him, he tries to be a pest and take them out of their comfort zone. "It's about having

Cavs forward Tristan Thompson drives between the Warriors' Andrew Bogut (left) and Draymond Green during Game 4 of the 2016 NBA Finals in Cleveland.

the heart," Thompson said. "I'm not going to back down. That's what my job is: do the little things and make guys uncomfortable."

"Backing down" is not in Thompson's vocabulary. "That's what I have to bring to this team," he said. "I bring toughness, energy. I can't back down from anybody. I have to bring it every night and accept the challenge."

Cavs coach David Blatt said he was fortunate to have a player of Thompson's caliber. "He's been very solid throughout the year," he said. "We're getting that maximum effort every time he steps on the floor. It's a big part of what he brings to the table and what we need from him."

Thompson spent the summer of 2015 embroiled in a contract dispute with the Cavs. He was a restricted free agent and reportedly turned down a five-year, $80 million deal in early July. He didn't sign until October 22, when he accepted a five-year, $82 million contract, agent Rich Paul told ESPN.com. Thompson, one of the league's best offensive rebounders, missed training camp and the entire preseason. He'll earn $16.4 million annually, which will make him the sixth-highest-paid power forward in the NBA. His contract equals the one signed by Golden State's Draymond Green.

85 Upgrading the Cavs' Defense

Every team seems to have a built-in scapegoat. In Cleveland, that man was Dion Waiters. Anything that seemed to go wrong on the Cavaliers, Waiters seemed to get the blame.

Cavaliers forward LeBron James wanted all of that to change. "I told Dion not to get involved in what people say about you," he said on media day in October 2014. "It's not what people think of you, it's about what you think of yourself. The only way to rewrite the notion of whether Dion can fit is to play the right way and dominate the opposition every night. That's all he should worry about."

Even though James didn't rejoin the Cavaliers until the summer of 2014, he'd heard all the scuttlebutt regarding the 6'4", 225-pound Waiters. "Can Dion play alongside Kyrie [Irving]?" he said. "When I came, can Dion take the role that D-Wade [Dwyane Wade] took? Is he a selfish player? Is he not a selfish player? Can he move without the ball? I'm not saying stuff that hasn't already been said."

James said he was going to take Waiters under his wing. "I will continue to stay on him," he said. "I want him to continue to learn the game mentally. Physically, he can be a very good player, if not a great player in our league. Our game is more mental than anything. If he can start thinking the game before he starts physically playing the game, he can be even more dynamic. I'm going to stay on him about that. The worst thing you can do is have him overthink the game."

Wizards guard Bradley Beal boasted that Washington's backcourt of him and John Wall is the best in the league. That rubbed Waiters the wrong way. Waiters thought it would be more accurate if Beal had mentioned Cleveland's starting backcourt of Kyrie Irving and Waiters. "That's nonsense," Waiters said. "He's supposed to say that. I know deep down, he's not messing with me and Ky. I think me and Ky have the best backcourt."

James said he thinks the Cavaliers' backcourt has a very high ceiling. "Obviously, we know what Kyrie is capable of doing," he said. "I believe Dion can do some great things as well [with] his ability to shoot the ball, handle the ball, his strength, [and] his athleticism."

James said he has no qualms about Irving and Waiters working well together. "You have two guys who love the game of basketball," he said. "They are gym rats. Why not? It's not hard for him to mesh."

Waiters said he's building chemistry with James. "At the end of the day, I want him to take me under his wing," Waiters said. "He's been there. He's won championships. He's a proven player. He's the best player in the world. Why not learn from a guy like that? I'm like a sponge out there."

Then Cavaliers coach David Blatt said Waiters had made a positive impression on him. "He came back here in real good shape," he said. "His weight is down. His body fat is down. His form is better, due to the work he put in this summer. We hope and believe he'll be more consistent in everything he does."

There have been questions in the past about how well Waiters moves without the ball. "The way we're playing," Blatt said, "he and everyone else will move without the ball. I guarantee it."

Many thought Waiters' job in the 2014 preseason was to find his niche. He needed to fit in somewhere behind the Cavs' three star players—James, Irving, and Kevin Love.

Waiters, never one to lack confidence, said he belongs in that elite class. "At the end of the day, it's going to come up eventually," Waiters said. "I ain't worried about it. I just have to go out there and play my game. They're going to say Big Four at the end of the year, or Big Five. That's what comes with it. I like being that dark horse."

Unfortunately, that was the last thing the Cavs' brass wanted to hear him say. Waiters is a talented player, as his No. 4 overall selection in the 2012 NBA Draft attests. But on this team, he needed to play strong defense, not turn the ball over, be a playmaker, and be ready to catch-and-shoot.

Waiters said all the right things heading into the preseason. He said players have to find a way to impact the game on defense. "At the end of the day, everyone has to take the challenge of guarding their man and buckling down on the defensive end," he said. "You can only try your best. The guys behind you have to have your back."

And then he went out and started jacking up shots in the 2014 preseason. Part of the reason was that the Big Three missed games. "I just take what's given to me," he said. "A lot of times guys will be out. That's more opportunities for me. I've got to be aggressive. That's me. That's who I am. But I'm not going to do anything to hurt the team. If I feel I'm shooting too much, I'm going to look for guys and try to play the game different ways."

Blatt said he had noticed the shot discrepancy. "I don't think he should lead the team in shots," he said. "On the other hand, I don't really care. I just want us to take good shots, and make them. It's something we really should look at, and we will."

James, Love, and Irving have 17 appearances in the All-Star Game between them. Waiters hasn't even sniffed an All-Star nod. He said he appreciates the praise that's been coming from James.

"It makes me work that much harder just knowing that somebody sees the talent," he said. "[It's great] just being around a guy like that who has been through it all. He's a proven winner. He's someone I can talk to."

Waiters said he'd have no problem playing in big games. "You know me," he said. "I love the bright lights. I don't shy away from those moments. I embrace them. I'm ready."

Irving suffered from a sprained right ankle. Waiters said he'd love to play point guard. "Over time, if I play point guard, I think I'd excel," he said. "I'd like the opportunity if the coach would give me a chance."

At the time, though, the Cavaliers were just trying to get a good feel for one another. They knew there would be much hype being one of the contenders for an NBA title. "We know what's at stake," Waiters said. "If you lose two or three games, it's going to seem like the end of the world. We just have to be ready for that. We have to know how to control it."

He said he got a head's up from James about a week before the latter made Decision 2.0 in July 2014. However, at the time, he said he didn't realize it. "We had talked in a regular conversation," Waiters said. "He told me to stay ready. 'Be ready.' He said he hadn't made up his mind on a decision yet. I was working out when I found out. I was more excited for the city more than anything. I think they deserve it."

Waiters wasn't around for the Cavs' stretch run to the NBA Finals. He was traded to Oklahoma City on January 5, 2015, in a three-team trade with New York. The Cavs sent forward Louis Amundson, center Alex Kirk, and a second-round pick to the Knicks. The Cavs received swingman J.R. Smith and shooting guard Iman Shumpert from the Knicks, and a first-round pick from the Thunder. Shumpert was billed as a lockdown defender when he burst upon the scene. He's done nothing to dispute that notion.

Without much fanfare and with little publicity, he had one of his best all-around games of the season in the 127–94 annihilation of the Dallas Mavericks on March 10, 2015. Shumpert finished with seven points, four rebounds, six assists, and six steals in 32 minutes.

Shumpert doesn't have to score a lot of points to make an impression. "We said after the game, 'I don't know how many points he scored, and I don't care,'" Cavaliers coach David Blatt told reporters after the Dallas game. "He impacted that game in so many ways tonight, and good for him."

The six steals tied a career high for the 6'5", 220-pound Shumpert. "That's what he brings to our team," Cavaliers forward LeBron James told Cavs.com. "I don't care about his scoring. I don't care if he scores [another] basket the rest of the season. All I care is how he defends, his aggressiveness, and being able to defend multiple positions. He's doing a great job of making shots when they come to him. But defensively is where he makes his mark. I know that from going against him in New York. We're happy to have him."

The Georgia Tech product defends the top perimeter threats on the opposing team. "Someone has to do it," Shumpert said. "We have a lot of guys who can do a lot of things. At times, you want to do other things, but you can't do them. Sometimes, you don't have the ball in your hands. I'm a young guy with a ton of energy. I might as well use it."

He is a true student of the game. He studies the opposing players' tendencies on video before each game. He goes so far as to count their dribbles before they pull up and pass the ball. Shumpert tries to disrupt their passing lanes and utilizes his good natural instincts.

"It's a collection of things," Shumpert said. "[I try to figure out] what I would do or what Kyrie [Irving] would do. I play offense on defense."

86 Trip to Stark County

The Cavs were one of the first NBA teams to have their own Development League franchise. Their D-League team, the Canton Charge, play their home games at the Canton Memorial Civic Center, 1101 Market Avenue North, Canton, Ohio. It holds about 5,000 fans. It offers pro basketball fans an affordable option to the high-priced tickets in the NBA.

It's also minor league basketball. The D-League was supposed to be like Triple A in baseball—a place to groom your prospects. It just hasn't turned out that way at all. Teams seem reluctant to send any of their top prospects to the D-League. They figure the players will get more out of practicing against NBA talent than they would going against other D-League players.

"We pride ourselves on being an extension of Cleveland, like a 'mini Cavs,' if you will," senior vice president/COO Mike Levy said. "The atmosphere for a game at The Q is incredible, and why wouldn't we want to have some of that for our fans in Canton, too?"

The Charge has been in existence since 2011. It's located about an hour south of downtown Cleveland. "We spend a lot of time in

Cleveland before the season starts getting to know the players and the system," Charge coach Jordi Fernandez said. "When our guys or Cavs players are with us in Canton, it feels exactly how it does in an NBA practice, and that attitude translates to our level of play."

"Wrong Way" Warren

The Cavaliers were so bad during their inaugural season in 1970–1971, they were the butt of many jokes.

Guard John Warren helped perpetuate that reputation on December 9, 1970, during a game against Portland at Cleveland Arena. Center Walt Wesley controlled the jump ball to start the third quarter. He tipped it to guard Bobby Lewis, who fed Warren for a layup.

There was only one problem. It was at the wrong basket.

What made the play even more hilarious was that Trail Blazers center Leroy Ellis tried to block the shot. "All I know is that I started running, and Ellis was right with me," Warren said.

Lewis was impressed with his nifty bounce pass to a streaking Warren. "I looked up and saw Johnny going," he said. "In fact, I had to make a super pass to get it to him."

Later in the game, the Blazers had six men on the court. They were slapped with a technical. Cavs coach Bill Fitch said while watching game film of Warren's play the next day, Cavs guard Bobby "Bingo" Smith caught some grief from his teammates. "He was waving his arms and screaming for the ball," Fitch said.

88 Amaechi Comes Out

Long before Jason Collins, there was NBA journeyman John Amaechi. Amaechi was the first NBA player to admit he was gay.

Amaechi played five NBA seasons, starting with the Cavs in 1995–1996. Four years after his retirement, in 2007, he made the shocking announcement. Nets forward/center Jason Collins followed suit in 2013.

"It was difficult living with this secret," Amaechi said. "Now it's like a tremendous weight has been lifted." He broke the news in his autobiography *Man in the Middle.*

LeBron James was quoted in an ESPN story that he didn't think an openly gay person could survive in the NBA. "With teammates you have to be trustworthy, and if you're gay and you're not admitting that you are, then you are not trustworthy," James said. "So that's like the No. 1 thing as teammates—we all trust each other. You've heard of the in-room, locker room code. What happens in the locker room stays in there. It's a trust factor, honestly. A big trust factor."

Amaechi made the Cavs team as an undrafted free agent from Penn State.

"It's a daunting task," he said.

89 Magic Happens at Akron General

Two of the NBA's brightest stars—Cavaliers forward LeBron James and Warriors point guard Stephen Curry—met in the 2015 NBA Finals. It was a matchup of a four-time Most Valuable Player in James versus the league's 2015 winner in Curry.

There was another interesting similarity: they were both born in Summa Akron City Hospital in Akron, Ohio, 39 months apart. LeBron Raymone James was born to Anthony McClelland and Gloria Marie James on December 30, 1984. Wardell Stephen Curry II was born to Dell and Sonya Curry on March 14, 1988.

Dell Curry played just one season with the Cavs in 1987–1988, and that's when his famous son was born. The Cavs mistakenly failed to protect him in the expansion draft the following year and lost him to the Charlotte Hornets. The sharpshooter, a trait he passed down to his son, played the next 10 years in Charlotte.

Steph Curry told reporters if scouts were smart, they'd be patrolling the hospital's maternity ward looking for potential prospects. "Every time I look at my birth certificate, it says Akron, Ohio," Steph said. "I think I was there maybe six months."

The delivery staff at Akron City Hospital has started calling it "the basketball center of the universe." "If you want your kid to be an NBA player, have them delivered here at Summa," said Dr. Edward Ferris, residency director and vice chair of obstetrics and gynecology at Summa Akron City Hospital.

James said he thought it was "pretty cool" that both he and Curry were born in the same hospital. "It's the true definition of a small world, for sure," he said.

90 Kevin Ollie: One of the Nicest Cavs

The Cavs had some injuries at the point guard position during the 2003–2004 season, and they were forced to play Kevin Ollie major minutes. He struggled in that role. Going against starting point guards, he was at a disadvantage. He was best-suited in a backup role against backup players.

The Cavs lost a game, which prompted Cavs coach Paul Silas to say, "You can't make chicken salad out of chicken shit." It was a swipe at the front office for the talent on the roster, and more specifically at Ollie.

I did a follow-up on the story the next day, criticizing Ollie's play. Of course, he certainly landed on his feet at UConn. He replaced Jim Calhoun as the Huskies' coach and went on to win an NCAA championship in 2014.

I remember vividly the story I wrote. I said he wasn't getting the job done, and the Cavs need to find a replacement. The next day I showed up and walked into the Cavs' locker room. Ollie was the only player in the locker room. He called me over. I walked over with my head down, knowing what was coming. He was going to get in my grill about what I had written.

"How was your Easter?" he asked. "Did you get to spend Easter with your family?"

I stumbled around for the right words.

"Uh, yes," I replied.

"It's a blessed holiday," he said. "Spending it with your family is important."

I felt about two inches tall. I felt terrible. I thought he was going to yell at me. Instead, he showed what a class act he was.

The Gatling Gun

The Cavs have had some real characters through the years. How about Derrick Chievous, the Band-Aid man? He would wear Band-Aids for no apparent reason. He just liked people to ask him what was wrong.

There was Tim Kempton, who could eat an entire Whopper from Burger King in one bite. How about Drew Gooden, who was bald, but had a square Soul patch of hair on the back of his head?

Then there was Chris Gatling. He spent 74 games with the Cavs during the 2000–2001 season after coming over from Miami in the Shawn Kemp trade. Cavs GM Jim Paxson finally found a taker for Kemp's massive contract. Paxson sent Kemp to Portland. The Cavs acquired three players—Gatling and Clarence Weatherspoon from Miami and Gary Grant from the Trail Blazers. Grant, a Canton (Ohio) McKinley High School product, was waived before he played a minute for the team.

The 6'10" Gatling could put the ball in the basket. He was a left-handed shooter. He showed very little interest in doing anything else. He was a very engaging fellow. If you walked by him in the locker room, he was taken aback if you didn't stop and interview him.

"You need anything?" he'd ask.

I've never witnessed a guy like that. Many players talk to the media grudgingly. Gatling was just the opposite. When we approached the trade deadline in February, his name was bandied about throughout the league. The Cavs shopped him heavily, hoping to acquire some young talent or a draft pick. He wasn't dealt, however, and finished out the season with the Cavs. He played in Russia the following year.

Once the deadline had passed, the "Gatling Gun" brought a large sheet cake into the locker room in celebration of not being traded. He cut generous pieces of cake and distributed them to the media when they entered the locker room. That was the first time that ever happened, and it will probably be the last.

That season, Randy Wittman's first as head coach, he described a game by Weatherspoon as a "yeoman's effort." *Cleveland Plain Dealer* reporter Mary Schmitt Boyer asked Weatherspoon after the game if he knew what it meant.

"I did go to college, Mary," he said snidely.

She kept her distance from him the rest of the season.

The Cleveland Presidents

In 1970 the *Cleveland Plain Dealer* held a name-the-team contest. Eastlake, Ohio, resident Jerry Tomko came up with the winning entry with "Cavaliers."

He won a pair of season tickets for the Cavs' first season at Cleveland Arena in 1970–1971. Tomko's essay read, "The name Cleveland Cavaliers represents a group of daring, fearless men whose life pact was never surrender, no matter what the odds."

Fans voted on five finalists, including Cavaliers, Presidents, Jays, Towers, and Foresters. More than one-third of the 6,000 fans who voted went with Cavaliers.

"I can't wait until the season starts, and I've already had people coming to me and asking me if they can use the tickets for some games," Tomko said on April 5, 1970.

As a footnote to the story, his son, Brett, was born almost three years to the day—on April 7, 1973—after the story ran in the Cleveland paper. A right-handed pitcher, Brett Tomko had a record of 100–103 in 14 seasons in the major leagues, most notably with the Cincinnati Reds.

Cavs' GM: Stand by Your Man

Cavs general manager David Griffin was tired of all the stories about coach David Blatt's job security. It was time to make a stand for his coach during an impromptu press conference on January 4, 2015.

"This narrative of our coaching situation is truly ridiculous," Griffin said. "It is a non-story, it's a non-narrative. Coach Blatt is our coach. He's going to remain our coach. Do not write that as a vote of confidence. He never needed one. It was never a question. So don't write it that way. I heard the entire audio file of LeBron James' comments. No more than three different times, he said, 'We are growing together every day,' 'The team grows together every day,' and 'I am happy with who we have at the helm.' But that wasn't a sexy pull quote, so we kept looking for something else until we could pull something that sounded negative. That narrative is done. No change is being made. Period."

Several stories had surfaced that Blatt's job was in jeopardy. The team was struggling to come together as a cohesive unit. "Growth and development and the long haul is what this is about," Griffin said. "Every member of our organization from top to bottom—ownership, myself, the players, the coaches, LeBron himself—signed on for the long haul. This is something we're doing over time. And yes, we've had some bumps. We've had it look really, really bad at times. Guys, this is a really difficult recipe to get right. Everybody needs to just settle down and let it happen. But I can promise you that's not a narrative that has validity at all, nor will it."

Griffin said he needed to speak up. All the negative stories were apparently eating at him. "Truthfully, if I wasn't speaking now I wouldn't feel like something needed to be said because it's just such a ridiculous assertion," the GM said. "It seemed giving life to it is what would happen by talking about it. So I didn't want to do that. At the same time, it's just time for everybody to get on with it. We have a chance to galvanize ourselves and grow and move in a positive direction. So I just want to make sure we're doing that in a fresh environment."

The media attempted to drag LeBron James into the Blatt controversy, but he kept them at arm's length. "I don't pay no bills around here, man," James said. "Listen, man, I play. I'm happy who we have at our helm. He's our coach."

He emphasized that he and Blatt have a good relationship. "To make it a feud between me and Blatt or the team and Blatt, it's just a sell," James said. "That's all it is: to get someone to read it and to put something on the bottom of the ticker. That's all it is. My relationship with the coach continues to get better day by day. This is two months of us being together. I don't know him fully. He doesn't know me fully. He doesn't know any of the guys fully, and that's to be expected. He has our attention. We know what we want to do out on the floor. We have to do a better job of executing what they want us to do, and do it at a high level."

James was asked if Blatt is the right coach for the team. "He's our coach," he said. "What other coach do we have? We have Coach Blatt and we have our assistants."

The Cavs selected Blatt as their coach on June 20, 2014. They signed the former Maccabi Tel Aviv coach to a three-year, $10 million contract, a league source said. The fourth year of the deal had a team option worth about $3.5 million to $4 million. There were also incentives in the deal to potentially make it more lucrative.

"David Blatt is going to bring some of the most innovative approaches found in professional basketball anywhere on the globe,"

Cavs majority owner Dan Gilbert said. "Time and time again, from Russia to Israel and several other prominent head-coaching jobs in between, David has done one thing: win. He is not only an innovator, well-trained and focused on both sides of the court, but he is always learning and always teaching. Whether you are a top draft pick just entering the league, or a seasoned NBA veteran, Coach Blatt is going to take your game and the game of the team you are playing for to a new and higher level."

Blatt, 55, emerged as the leader in the coaching search on June 19, nudging out the highly regarded Tyronn Lue, an assistant coach with the Los Angeles Clippers. Lue was hired as his associate head coach on his staff in Cleveland.

Blatt is the first coach to move from Europe to become a head coach in the NBA. He was the Cavs' 20th head coach in franchise history, replacing Mike Brown, who was fired on May 12, 2014. "I couldn't be more excited about the opportunity to come to Cleveland and lead the Cavaliers as their head coach," Blatt said. "After spending a great deal of time discussing the organization, the team and the head coach's role with David Griffin, I feel strongly about my fit for the job and this team's potential. This is an opportune time to join the Cleveland Cavaliers. We are going to work extremely hard to achieve the kind of results we all expect and know are possible. This is a proud day for me, personally, but I hope just the first of many more for all of us as we work towards a very bright future. I have always heard about how great of a sports town Cleveland is and have come to understand how much fans here care about the Cavaliers. This makes me feel especially excited and comfortable to join this community, but above all motivates me to help deliver in a big way."

The hiring was lauded all over the league. "He's the real deal," CBS basketball analyst Doug Gottlieb said. "People couldn't be more effusive in their praise [of him]." Gottlieb said when he played in Israel, Blatt was an assistant coach on the team and that if there was a negative, it was that Blatt is "wired to win." "He's always on," he said. "He's always thinking of ways to try to improve. He has an incredible background."

Another source who saw him coach in Europe for years said he's an intense competitor. He thinks nothing of yelling at his players, something that doesn't fly in the NBA. "His temperament has to change," he said.

Blatt had never coached a game in the NBA. The Boston native played at Princeton for legendary coach Pete Carril. However, he coached overseas for more than 20 years, including head-coaching stints in Israel, Greece, Russia, and Turkey. He coached perennial Euroleague championship contender Maccabi Tel Aviv, where his team finished with a 54–18 record in 2013–2014, winning the Israel League, Israeli Cup, and the Euroleague championship. Over the past four seasons, Blatt's teams went 225–55 (.804), including a team-best 70–13 record in 2011–2012.

"David is a great basketball coach and a special person," Griffin said. "His abilities to communicate, to build relationships with his players, and to foster winning environments at several stops throughout Europe and across the highest levels of international competition speaks for itself. He brings unbridled passion, energy, and creativity to his craft. These qualities have enabled David to reach a level of success that is truly unique."

Griffin, who spearheaded the Cavs' five-week coaching search, said he thought Blatt would have a smooth transition to the NBA. "There is a great opportunity to accelerate the progress of moving our team and franchise to the higher level of play we all believe we are capable of achieving," he said. "I am excited that the experience, knowledge, skills, and leadership David will bring to the Cavaliers is the right fit at the right time."

Blatt bristled when he was referred to as a "rookie" coach. He reminded everyone he's been coaching for more than 20 years. The Cavaliers presented Blatt with a game ball for his first NBA coaching win on October 31, 2014, in Chicago.

"Welcome to the NBA, Coach Blatt," Cavs forward/center Tristan Thompson said. "He got his first win. Let's get another one Tuesday [in Portland]."

Blatt said he received an interesting note from one of his friends after the Bulls game. "'That's wonderful,'" it said. "'Great job on your first win. Make sure it's not your last.'"

Cavs guard Kyrie Irving gave Blatt the game ball. "The team will have it embroidered," Blatt said. "It was moving. It was a beautiful thing."

Two weeks into the 2014–2015 regular season, he returned to his old stomping grounds for the Boston Celtics game on November 14 at TD Garden. Blatt, the newly minted Cavs coach, grew up in Framingham, Massachusetts, 20 miles west of Boston. He listened to Hall of Fame announcer Johnny Most doing Celtics games with a transistor radio pressed to his ear. "It'll be special for him to return there," Cavs forward LeBron James said. "I'm sure he'll have some friends and family there. As a head coach in the NBA, it's probably a dream of his to be back. It'll be pretty awesome."

Blatt admitted the game was emotional for him. "[It's] kind of special," he said. "But [it's] nothing that's going to keep me from doing my job to the best of my ability."

He was a huge Celtics fan while growing up. "Bill Russell was my childhood hero," Blatt said. "He was my idol."

However, his allegiances have changed. Blatt said he never dreamt of coaching in the Garden. "Not when I was growing up," he said. "I never imagined I would be either coaching or coaching in the NBA. But I did want to be in the NBA. Those days I was playing. I lived in the Boston area until I graduated from college [Princeton], and then I left. That was 33 years ago. So it's been quite some time. But a lot of fond memories of the area, of the people, and of the NBA game that I grew to love through following the Celtics."

Blatt had no trouble reverting back to his old Boston accent. "That left with me leaving the United States 33 years ago," he said.

"It's easy for me to fall back into it, but it's gone now that I've managed to move on. See, I speak four languages, but 17 dialects. I've been a lot of different places. Boston talk is easy for me."

It was quite obvious he was highly intelligent. After all, he was an English literature major at Princeton. While talking about an injured player on December 14, 2014, at Cleveland Clinic Courts, he informed the media he wasn't a doctor. But he was surrounded by several of them in his life. "My dad was a doctor of biochemistry," he said. "My wife is a doctor of economics. I'm just a basketball coach. I have two older sisters who were of a genius IQ. My parents always told me I was at the low end of the gene pool in the family."

Blatt spent much of his first season with the Cavs massaging the English language. It began when reporters were asking about his decision to send Dion Waiters to the bench. "We didn't bench Dion," Blatt said with a straight face. "He's the sixth starter."

Let's not forget about when the Cavaliers re-signed guard A.J. Price. Price made the team out of camp, got waived in favor of Will Cherry, and then was brought back.

"Why did you get rid of Price in the first place?" Blatt was asked.

"That's a little harsh," Blatt said. "We didn't get rid of him. We waived him."

Then, after veteran swingman Mike Miller recorded three consecutive Did Not Play–Coach's Decisions, he appeared in a game against Milwaukee.

"Is Mike Miller back in the rotation?" Blatt was asked.

"He never left the rotation," he said. "He was just taking a little break."

Another time, Blatt was tired of the line of questioning about Kevin Love not playing in the fourth quarter. "You guys jump on every little thing I say, and it becomes a headline," he said. "I'm not going to say anything anymore. There are so many knee-jerk reactions. This will probably cause another one."

Finally, after Game 1 of the playoffs, Blatt was at the podium, built up about three feet off the floor. He was looking down on the media.

"You can say I like to look down on all of you," he joked.

Blatt was fired as Cavs coach January 22, 2016.

94 "Dinner Bell" Mel Turpin

The 1984 NBA Draft was one of the best ever. Several future Hall of Famers and all-time greats were available, including Michael Jordan, Charles Barkley, Hakeem Olajuwon, and John Stockton. The Cavs, who had the sixth overall pick, didn't get their hands on any of them.

Cleveland sent Tim McCormick, Cliff Robinson, and cash to the Washington Bullets on June 19, 1984, for the rights to the No. 6 pick. The deal was announced on draft night, but was arranged much earlier.

The Cavs' personnel department had their sights set on Barkley, Auburn's "Round Mound of Rebound." Unfortunately, Philadelphia beat them to the punch at No. 5. "We made the trade with the hope that Charles Barkley would drop to six," Cavs coach George Karl said. "We didn't get lucky. And then we had to take the player who we thought was the next-best player available in that draft."

That was Kentucky's Melvin Turpin, a 6'11" center. Karl was named head coach and made a habit of criticizing the fleshy rookie. Karl openly questioned Turpin's work ethic. "Dinner Bell" Mel was listed at 260 pounds, but many thought he was actually pushing 300.

"George thought 'Dinner Bell' could play," *Cleveland Plain Dealer* beat writer Burt Graeff said. "He felt it was a waste of talent.

Mel could really shoot. He was not a great post-up player." In three seasons with the Cavs, Turpin averaged 10.4 points and 5.4 rebounds.

Former Kentucky teammate Kenny "Sky" Walker told the *Lexington Herald Leader* that Turpin was "a loveable giant, a guy who always had a smile on his face. Everybody who played with him absolutely adored him."

He was jovial—and in many ways lovable. He signed a three-year contract for $1 million, but reportedly paid $90,000 in fines for being overweight his first season. It got to the point where he would just pay the fines instead of stepping on the scales. Turpin weighed 287 pounds when he was traded by the Cavs to Utah in 1987. Inexplicably, he weighed in at 301 when he arrived in Salt Lake City a few days later.

"What can I say? I love airline food," he told the Jazz trainer.

The Turpin selection can be blamed on bad luck. The circumstances surrounding the selection of Keith Lee in 1985, however, were nothing short of a disaster. First, they left Hall of Fame power forward Karl Malone on the board and wanted to get their hands on Lee—a Memphis standout—with the No. 13 overall pick. They worked out both Malone and Lee heading up to the draft. In fact, they had Malone go one-on-one against Turpin in his workout.

"If I had any doubts about playing in the NBA, they ended then," he said.

The Cavs ended up drafting Charles Oakley and trading him to Chicago for the rights to Lee and guard Ennis Whatley on June 18, 1985. Had they drafted Malone or just kept Oakley, it would have been a huge acquisition for the Cavs.

Instead, Lee was a 6.7-point scorer in two uneventful seasons with the team.

Turpin, meanwhile, died at age 49 in 2010 of a self-inflicted gunshot wound.

95 Thrill of Being on the Road

Traveling around the United States and Canada covering the Cavs is certainly a perk for any job. I got to see the country, at least the cities with NBA venues. But it wasn't always as glamorous as many people thought. There were those days that you'd just like to forget.

I was having one of those days while trying to get to Miami. My flight from Cleveland was delayed. Sitting around in airports was part of the job. There's always work to be done, so I pulled out my laptop and waited for the flight to leave. I finally got on the plane and got to Miami. I made it through the Miami airport and found my shuttle to the rental car agency.

It was hot and muggy. I could feel sweat running down my back. Tensions grew when I got inside the office and there was a line 10 deep. I asked for a mid-size car, but they were sold out (of course). Finally, they found something with four wheels, and I jumped on it.

The paperwork took longer than usual, but I finally got out of there. All I could think of was getting some lunch and taking a short nap before going to AmericanAirlines Arena that evening for the game. When I hopped in the car, I looked at the gas gauge, and it was half full. That was the last straw. I called over one of the rental car attendants and got in his grill.

"Is it too much to ask that you give me a car with a full tank of gas?" I said rudely, pointing to the gas gauge.

The attendant stuck his head in my driver's side window.

"Sir, that's the temperature gauge," he replied.

At that point, I felt like a complete dope. I thanked him for his help and sped off.

One other time, I was at my hotel and just getting out of the shower in the morning. For some reason, I had forgotten to dead-bolt the door. I was walking out of the bathroom in my birthday suit, and the door opened. I instinctively put my hand out to stop the door from opening. The room attendant's forehead bounced off the door as it slammed shut.

Not good.

I quickly got dressed, as there was a loud knock on the door. When I answered it, it was a supervisor, wondering why I had assaulted the attendant, who happened to be deaf. I apologized for my behavior—and left a big tip in my room.

Perhaps the worst road trip I had ever taken came for Game 5 of the 2015 NBA Finals. The day started with a cab to the San Francisco International Airport at about 8:00 AM. Upon arrival, I realized my flight was canceled for maintenance reasons. The line to get on the next flight—through Chicago—was a mile long. I called my travel agent, who booked me on a flight at 9:00 PM. I had to spend the entire day in the airport. You can only eat so many times.

About two hours before that flight, I walked to another terminal to that gate. They had no record of me on the flight. Every seat was taken. I have some elite status on United, which would help me in these cases. Unfortunately, I had none on American.

"How could this happen?" I asked my travel agent. "Sorry," she said.

She said there was one more flight out of SFO that would get me to Cleveland. That was supposed to leave at midnight. It was astronomically priced at $800 for the one-way trip. Game 6 was in Cleveland the next night. I thought I needed to be there, even though we had a fleet of writers, photographers, and videographers from our paper going to the game. I was the beat writer, and would be expected to write the main story and analysis after the game.

I finally made it down to the gate. United made a gate-change announcement. A whole group of travelers walked to the new gate.

They soon made the announcement that that flight was going to be canceled.

This can't be happening.

I waited at the service counter for almost three hours before I got to the front of the line. They moved me to a flight that left at 1:00 PM the next day, nonstop to Cleveland. They graciously gave me a coupon for a hotel. Unfortunately, every room was filled. I had to spend the night in the airport.

I remembered seeing a couch halfway down the corridor. When I arrived, some guy was sound asleep on it. I did find a chair and tried to sleep. It wasn't happening. I finally sprawled out on the floor, with my computer bag under my head, and went to sleep. It was one of the worst nights of my life.

I made it back to Cleveland on the night of the game. I think the game started when I touched down at Cleveland Hopkins International Airport. By the time I made it to The Q, I missed the entire first quarter.

The Cavs ended up losing the game and the series, but I slept like a rock when I finally got home around 2:30 AM.

96 The Streak

After losing LeBron James to free agency, things bottomed out for the Cavaliers in 2010–2011. Coach Byron Scott's club lost 26 games in a row, which tied the longest streak in NBA history. The Cavs went from winning 61 games in 2009–2010 to just 19 in 2010–2011. It was the biggest drop in wins ever in back-to-back seasons in the NBA.

The streak started with a 101–90 setback to the Utah Jazz on December 20, 2010. They didn't experience the thrill of victory again until they upended the Los Angeles Clippers 126–119 in two overtimes on February 11, 2011. Before the losing streak started, they had just lost 10 in a row before defeating New York in overtime on December 18, 109–102. So, in actuality, they lost 36 of 37 games during that stretch.

The Philadelphia 76ers later tied that dubious record with 26 consecutive losses during the 2013–2014 season.

After they beat the Clippers, the Cavs players were beaming in the postgame locker room. "I can smile again," Cavs guard Daniel "Boobie" Gibson said. "It feels pretty good. Winning is a precious feeling."

Scott had criticized the team after a lackluster effort against Detroit on February 9. He said he was "mad as hell."

Getting back on the winning track cured all their ills. "We finally got the monkey off our back," he said. "I expect our guys to play this hard every single night. If we do that, we'll be okay."

97 Five Wives

Christian Eyenga was such an unknown quantity when the Cavs selected him in the first round of the 2009 draft, he wasn't even in the *NBA Draft Guide.*

For some inexplicable reason, Cavs general manager Danny Ferry used the 30th overall pick on the Republic of Congo native. The 6'5", 210-pounder could jump out of the gym and was extremely athletic, but was as raw as they come. He had no clue how to play the game. They brought him to the Cavs in 2010 and just dumped him in coach Byron Scott's lap.

He might not have been a great player, but he told some good stories. One night during the 2010–2011 season, he informed the media that his 73-year-old father had five wives.

I asked him if that is allowed in the Congo. He said, "Sure."

"I want five too," Eyenga said.

I asked if his dad spends time with one wife on Monday, one on Tuesday, and so on.

Eyenga said that's not the case. Some of the wives are mad at his father. Apparently, he's met a new lady friend. Eyenga said his father has so many children, he doesn't know how many he has. He also can't remember all of their names.

Upon further review, Eyenga changed his mind and said he doesn't want five wives, especially if he remains in the United States. "American women are crazy," he said.

Speaking of crazy, a man brandishing a knife made his way onto the Staples Center court an hour before the Cavs-Clippers game on March 19, 2011. Eyenga was on the court shooting. When he saw the man with the knife, he sprinted off the court and went back to the locker room for safety.

Coach Scott said Eyenga reacted the right way. "Smart man," Scott told the *Cleveland Plain Dealer*. "He understands *knife*, I guess. I think that goes all the way to Congo. Knife means get the hell out. So he did the right thing."

98 The Hot Dog Man

One of the strangest guys to ever play for the Cavs—and there have been many—was forward Gary Suiter. He did many odd things during his brief stint with the Cavs, but nothing was as zany as when he came up missing for their first game. They were in the pregame huddle waiting to play the Buffalo Braves on October 14, 1970, and he was nowhere in sight.

Coach Bill Fitch sent trainer Ron Culp to find the 6′9″, 235-pound Suiter. He located him standing in line at the concession stand wearing his warmup jersey. Suiter wanted a couple of hot dogs and a Coke before the game.

He ended up playing 30 uneventful games for the Cavs during their inaugural season. Fitch finally waived him after he was caught going through teammate Larry Mikan's luggage. Suiter would never appear in an NBA game again.

"The guy was strange," Cavs assistant coach Jim Lessig said.

Suiter was murdered in Rio Rancho, New Mexico, on October 23, 1982. He was only 37.

99 He's a Cleveland Treasure

One of the real success stories in Cleveland is the ascension of Michael Symon as a culinary icon. He describes himself as a husband and father, Iron Chef on the Food Network, and cohost of ABC's *The Chew*. Symon's empire in Cleveland is bulging at the seams, starting with Lola Bistro, 2058 East Fourth Street. Its menu offers diners a modern interpretation of their favorite midwestern dishes. Its website calls Lola the crown jewel of Cleveland's vibrant culinary scene. Lola will soon have a new neighbor, Mabel's BBQ, which will soon open on East Fourth. It's actually named after Symon's beloved bull mastiff, Mabel. It will be a barbecue joint, with Symon's signature twist. Another popular location is Lolita, 900 Literary Road, which is nestled in the chic Tremont neighborhood. It suffered significant fire damage in January 2016.

B Spot is a burger haven with several locations downtown and in the Greater Cleveland area. Its burgers have been voted best in America at the Sobe Burger Bash in 2010, 2011, 2012, and 2014.

There are sites at FirstEnergy Stadium's Club Lounge and Luxury Suites, and at Quicken Loans Arena in the Main Concourse near the Cavs Team shop. There are also B Spots in Westlake, Strongsville, and Beachwood in Greater Cleveland, as well as Columbus, Detroit, and Indianapolis.

Symon has opened Roast, 1128 Washington Boulevard, Detroit, which earned Hour Detroit Magazine's best steakhouse award. Bar Symon has also opened at Pittsburgh International Airport and Washington Dulles Airport. They deliver a menu of hearty comfort food for travelers to enjoy in a vibrant tap-house setting.

100 How Much Does LeBron Have Left in the Tank?

One can make a solid case that LeBron James is still the best overall player in the NBA. The question is, how many more years does he have at an elite level? Two? Three?

He has a lot of mileage on his body. By the end of the 2016 NBA Finals, he had played 199 career playoff games—the equivalent of almost two-and-a-half extra seasons. James is 31 years old.

He's one of eight players in history to play in the NBA Finals for six consecutive years (four in Miami, two in Cleveland). That hasn't happened in the NBA since several Boston Celtics did it last in 1966.

One thing in his favor is that he's never had a serious injury in the NBA. He did break his wrist after his junior year in high school. Since joining the NBA, he's had a few ankle sprains, problems with his elbow, and a few others that were probably never disclosed.

The four-time league MVP is closer to the end of his career than the beginning, but retirement is the furthest thing from his mind. He can probably play another eight or nine years if he wants, but he will no longer be considered the best player in the NBA.

LeBron James goes in for a dunk against Golden State during Game 6 of the 2016 NBA Finals.

That's not the case right now. Other players do certain things better. Golden State's Stephen Curry, two-time MVP, is a superior shooter, but he doesn't have the overall game that James possesses. James, a 10-time first-team All-NBA player, was asked during the 2016 playoffs how long he planned to keep playing.

"Later on in my thirties," he said. "It's kind of up to my kids, really. I miss so much of my kids' tournaments and things of that nature, it's kind of up to them. They'll let me know when they're tired of seeing me go away."

James and his wife, Savannah, have three children: 11-year-old LeBron Jr., eight-year-old Bryce Maximus, and 18-month-old daughter Zhuri.

Sources

Embry, Wayne, with Mary Schmitt Boyer. *Inside Game: Race, Power and Politics in the NBA*. Akron, Ohio: University of Akron Press, 2004.

Menzer, Joe, and Burt Graeff. *Cavs: From Fitch to Fratello: The Sometimes Miraculous, Often Hilarious Wild Ride of the Cleveland Cavaliers*. Urbana, Illinois: Sagamore Publishing, 1994.

Pluto, Terry, and Joe Tait. *Joe Tait: It's Been a Real Ball*. Cleveland: Gray & Company Publishers, 2011.